MUNICH to MONTREAL

Women's Olympic Swimming
in a Tarnished Golden Era

Casey Converse

Casey Converse (signature)

A portion of the proceeds from the sale of this book will benefit the USA Swimming Foundation and its mission to save lives and build champions—in the pool and in life. www.USASwimmingFoundation.org

Munich to Montreal: Women's Olympic Swimming in a Tarnished Golden Era

Copyright © 2016 by Casey Converse | www.MunichToMontreal.com
The author can be contacted at kcconverse@munichtomontreal.com.

ISBN 978-0-578-17852-3
2016—First Edition
Printed in the United States of America

Cover and Interior Design | Melissa Tenpas —www.MelissaTenpas.com
Cover Photograph | Courtesty of USA Swimming and
Rob Fortunato, Director of Photography—www.RobFortunato.com

CONTENTS

FOREWORD

LET'S BE CANDID: the chief purpose of any foreword is to tell a prospective reader why the author's work is worthy.

The author of this book screams the word *worthy*. He has lived the story you are about to read, from every possible perspective: as a swimming prodigy in the early seventies; as an Olympian in Montreal; as a champion competitor; as a distinguished coach who helped to nurture sports equality for women; as a motivator who has pushed his athletes to find the outer edge of what is possible.

To be clear, this story is not about the man who is writing it. It is not a memoir. What it is, rather, is a burning passion project that the author has felt a moral need to complete. Because, above all, this is a story about galling, unremedied injustice and astonishing, unconditional resolve. And the author wants the world to know that this injustice and this resolve should never be forgotten.

Casey Converse—or Coach Converse, as he is principally known to his swimmers at the Air Force Academy—has every credential imaginable to tell this story like no one has told it before.

His story as a competitor begins when, as a teenager, he bravely left Alabama for Southern California. This was an America when extreme culture shock was still possible and a trip from the Deep South to SoCal's raging hip and cool might as well have been a space voyage between distant stars.

At the same time, it was also a world more simply defined by the geography of a Cold War: Capitalist versus Communist, Us versus Them. We were right. They were wrong.

Casey made the journey to California in order to see how far he could stretch his incipient swimming talent. As he arrived at Los Angeles International Airport, he was met by one of the central figures of this story, Mark Schubert, who would eventually become the 8-time U.S. Olympic swim team coach. Schubert, one of a growing legion of transplants from the East, was creating a swim mecca in Mission Viejo.

While at Mission Viejo, Casey also swam in the same pool as another central figure of this book, the remarkable and irrepressible Shirley Babashoff.

Babashoff might be the greatest Olympic athlete who has both the most essential and least-known legacy. After her performance at the 1976 Montreal Olympics, and for that matter the three previous years of tenacious swimming against doped East German athletes, she should have earned a spot in the swimming pantheon with Mark Spitz and now Michael Phelps. How her rightful place in history was effectively stolen from her is something you will fully learn in this book.

At age 18, a high school senior, Casey joined Shirley Babashoff on the Montreal Olympic team. And his men's team—powered in part by a superlative core from the new collegiate power USC—is arguably the greatest Olympic team in any sport in the history of the modern Games. Moreover, Casey's Olympic coach was Indiana's Doc Counsilman, the sport's first great guru; the coach who'd guided Spitz to seven golds, the author of the first great training bible for swimmers.

Casey was already a four-time U.S. national champion when he returned to Alabama to swim for the Crimson Tide. As a freshman competing at the NCAA Championships, he earned a place in swimming history as the first to ever break 15 minutes in the mile. Such victories are years in the making, calculated in wearying workloads of thousands and thousands of laps, AM and PM, day after day.

This perpetual student of the sport never ceased his search for excellence, and like many everlasting learners he became a lifelong teacher. Today, he is approaching 30 years coaching at the Air Force Academy, on a campus dramatically perched amid the Rockies in Colorado Springs, Colorado. Here, a visitor to the pool is first struck by a sign with large block letters that advertises to opponents the lung-searing elevation at which they will be expected to compete:

The Air is Rare
7,250 feet

In 1995 and 1996, the Air Force women's team won back-to-back Division II NCAA Championships. The 1996 team set the all-time scoring record. And though high altitude may give Air Force athletes a slight home-field advantage, their frightening academic workload is, notably, rather consumptive, science on top of engineering on top of mathematics. Casey is equally proud—if not prouder—of what his cadets have done after graduation. In the first Gulf War, one of his swimmers became the first female pilot to be decorated for a combat mission. Another swimmer is about to return to the Academy as the head of the History Department.

I first met Coach a little over two years ago. It was over lunch in the cafeteria of the United States Olympic Committee Training Center, which is down the road from the Air Force Academy. At this particular cafeteria, you can't avoid the palpable electricity from the energy and intensity being emitted by young Olympic hopefuls of all sports, of all shapes and sizes … all ultimately united by their ravenous appetites, each wielding trays with copious amounts of food that they rapidly inhale before reloading.

I was lunching with Coach because, by coincidence, USA Swimming, under Chuck Wielgus and Mike Unger, had hired me to direct a documentary about this same time period. It's called *The Last Gold*. Knowing of Casey's book project, USA Swimming had logically asked him to serve as a consultant on the film.

If my view was top down, with a steep learning curve, his was bottom up, and very personal.

In witnessing the difficult and ongoing evolution of women's sports in America, Casey has gained a deep, emotional understanding of the struggle endured by Babashoff's pioneering generation, and those who've followed. But there was an even greater force impeding the women of the Montreal Olympic team: a win-at-all costs East German sports machine that was poisoning its young athletes for what would be victory in the short-term but, for many, horrific, long-term health issues. This was compounded, in the West, by a conspiracy of silence. No one in the swimming establishment was prepared to confront the increasingly obvious: that East Germany was running a very sophisticated doping industrial complex.

Coach Converse was with me and Mr. Unger when we rolled our first frames of the film. This was for a scenic shot of the vineyards surrounding the classically quaint village of Schornsheim, the current home of the star of the 1976 East German team, Kornelia Ender. On that same trip, we'd also visit the former East German town of Bitterfeld, where Ender was born and raised – and from which she departed long ago. For Casey, it was a chance to compare and contrast.

Bitterfeld is hardly a postcard destination: it's yet another example of the kind of drab, soulless uniformity built by a failed state, which came to determine that gold-medal performances at the Olympics might provide desperately-needed political legitimacy at home and abroad. In this saga, Ender, and her teammates, were victims, too; doped without their knowledge, or their consent. As Casey walked the sidewalks of Bitterfeld, remembering the bountiful sunshine of his California training days, the process of comparing and contrasting made it even clearer to him just how fortunate he was to be born in the USA.

While Casey was researching this book, and as I was doing the same as film director, we were able to play detective for each other. Pathological lying was the First Commandment of the East German state. Secrets were ruthlessly maintained. At the same time, the environment for American women's sports in the seventies was often fuzzy, improvisational, and even invisible.

Though this story is about a tragedy that lasted long after the Montreal Games, this is also a story about the triumph of the will. The 1976 American women's swim team did not go down without a fight. There are miracles in this story. As importantly, many of the central players—American and German—are people of enormous character, steadfast and shining; people who spoke truth to power with an extraordinary amount of courage.

It's about time we all really understood what truly happened from *Munich to Montreal*, and why that's important. Along with all of its Shakespearian elements, this is also a cautionary tale. And your very worthy author has spent a lifetime seeking to provide you with all the necessary details.

Brian T. Brown
February 2016

This book is dedicated to the 1976 USA Women's Olympic Swim Team.

Shirley Babashoff, Melissa Belote, Wendy Boglioli, Brenda Borgh, Lelei Fonoimoana, Maryanne Graham, Jeanne Haney, Janis Hape, Kathy Heddy, Jennifer Hooker, Linda Jezek, Nicole Kramer, Renee Laravie, Renee Magee, Marcia Morey, Kim Peyton, Laurie Siering, Mirium Smith, Jill Sterkel, Karen Thornton, Tauna Vandeweghe, Wendy Weinberg, Donnalee Wennerstrom, and Camille Wright

Your experience is unique in the history of the Olympic Games. I hope that each of you finds something of your own story in this book.

And to my mother, Dorothy Peterson Converse.

ACKNOWLEDGEMENTS

This book was improved and enhanced immeasurably by the developmental editing of Andrea Varney Jewell of To The Point Editing, Colorado Springs, Colorado. I cannot thank Andrea enough for her encouragement, her commitment to this story, her professional guidance and her friendship. Copy editing was done by Scott DeNicola, Colorado Springs. Book design by Melissa Tenpas, Colorado Springs.

Many thanks to:
Barb and Gene Peyton, Wendy Boglioli, Bernie Boglioli, Jill Sterkel, Enith Brigitha, Kathy [Heddy] Drum, Karen Moe Thornton, Jennifer [Hooker] Brenniger, Maryanne [Graham] Keever, Joanne Sterkel, Kari Lydersen, Karen Andrus, Dennis Baker, Brian Goodell, John Naber, Bill Palmer, Don LaMont, Jim and Bev Montrella, Mark Schubert, Chuck Warner, Peter and Ingrid Daland, Don Gambril, Jack Nelson and Sherrill Nelson, Anne Goodman James, Jack Simon, Jay Fitzgerald, Dennis Pursley, Jack Ridley, Randy Reese, John Leonard, USAF Brigadier General Mark Wells, USAF Captain Robin Cadow, Research Staff of the McDermott Library of the United States Air Force Academy, USA Swimming, Chuck Wielgus, Mike Unger, Amanda Bryant, Joel Staufer, Larry Herr, Swimming World Magazine, Brent Reutmiller, Richard Deal, Bob Ingram International Swimming Hall of Fame, Bruce Wigo, Ivone Schmid, Sheila Roberston, Cathy Drozda, Jenny Stewart, Cassie Dixon, Chris Bramer, and Rob Fortunato

Early readers:
Lori Shumate, Dan Stephenson, Brian T. Brown, Chuck Wielgus, Mike Unger, Chuck Warner, Jay Fitzgerald, John Leonard, Brent Reutemiller, Kathie Wickstrand, Karen Crouse, and the Colorado Springs non-fiction writers meet-up group

Those who had to hear about "the book" and "goggles" for [at least] 4 years:
Rosie, Maggie, Tito, Joey, Colleen, and the USAFA Women's Swim Team

INTRODUCTION

THE STORY OF THE USA'S WOMEN'S SWIM TEAM at the 1976 Montreal Olympics has nagged at me for a very long time. In a box on my desk is an ancient looking 3x5 note card with the split times of both the USA swimmers and the East German swimmers who raced each other in the 4x100 freestyle relay in Montreal. The card is dog-eared and yellowed from age. It may be twenty years ago or more since I made those first notes. The story of "The Great Race", so called by Bernie Boglioli is one of the great stories of the modern Olympic Games.

Along the way, I have done my best to learn eanough about the history of Germany to provide a sense of the geo-political backdrop of the 1970's. [Many, many thanks to the generosity of USA Swimming, Chuck Wielgus, Mike Unger, and Amanda Bryant for providing access to interviews for the film documentary *The Last Gold*—without those resources this book would probably have never been completed].

As much as anything I have tried to illuminate the obstacles that the women of the 1976 Olympic swim team overcame— most of which were not faced by their male counterparts. As the author I realize that some editorializing is unavoidable, but I tried to stay out of the story as much as possible. Some friends and readers familiar with this era of swimming will know that I swam on the Mission Viejo swim team in 1975 and 1976, and was a member of the 1976 men's Olympic team in Montreal. Some of the memories in the book are mine. For instance, I am the third swimmer in the lane with Brian Goodell and Shirley Babashoff in the story of the April '76 swim practice where Shirley swam two seconds over the existing World Record in a set of 3x800 meters freestyle.

Finally, I feel compelled to apologize to the USA women Olympians from 1976. Personally, as an 18 year-old male, I was utterly oblivious to the situation in Montreal. And I do not remember even one conversation in which anyone, from my own coach Mark Schubert to our Olympic coaches and teammates where the situation facing our women's team was discussed. In my memory there was no discussion of East German drug use, or the unfair disadvantage that was facing the USA women's team.

I began writing this book in the fall of 2012. It was in this time-frame that the conspiracy of silence that surrounded American Tour de France champion Lance Armstrong began to crumble. In October of that year, Armstrong was stripped of his record 7 Tour de France Titles, a sanction he chose not to appeal. While the details of doping at the 1976 Olympic Games in Montreal are very different, the Armstrong story brings home the truth that the battle for clean sport is never ending. The personal history of my own family intersected this event with the arrival of my first grandson, Jace in the same month.

Bookending the Armstrong disgrace and the completion of this manuscript four years later, was the news in late 2015 that Russian track and field athletes had been sanctioned by the World Anti Doping Agency after a thorough investigation into what was referred to as the "industrial scale" use of performance enhancing drugs. With six months to go before the opening ceremonies in Rio, it is not clear if Russian track athletes will be allowed to compete at the 2016 Games. Again, on a personal level, my second grandson Manolo was born around the same time in Medford Oregon.

In light of Montreal, Armstrong, and the Russian Track scandal, it would be easy to say cynically, that the more things change, the more they stay the same. But in fact, things have changed. Without the policing of Olympic sport by the World Anti Doping Agency, formed in 1999, the chance that doped Russian track and field athletes would have competed in the 2016 Rio Games undetected is almost certain. The results of the Montreal Olympics can never be reclaimed, but in Rio at least, it appears the Olympic Games has averted a repeat of a dark era in its history.

Which brings me back to my two grandsons. At the conclusion of each Olympic Games the head of the International Olympic Committee, calls for the "youth of the world" to assemble again in four years at the next Olympic host city.

The notion of fair play in sport, from little league to the Olympic Games is critical. One of the tenants of sport that makes it compelling to athletes and fans is the idea of the "uncertain outcome". If the outcome of a game or race is decided ultimately by which athletes have access to the best pharmacology, the essence of sport is in danger of being lost. If performance-enhancing drugs are not diligently policed by a unified worldwide athletics community, Olympic sport is in peril.

The "youth of the world"; Jace and Manolo, and all of our children and grandchildren may lose the opportunity to learn the inherent lessons earned through clean sport. Focused work, attention to detail, perseverance, these elemental human endeavors, tested and proven in real-time through sport, are in danger of being stolen by the results-skewing invasion of performance-enhancing drugs. For the sake of the children I hope we will remain diligent in supporting clean sport.

Chapter 1

THE ANIMALS

The story of Mark Schubert's first practice with swimmer Shirley Babashoff has been told and retold. After the practice Schubert had gone home and written the hardest practice he could think of—only to have Babashoff and her training partners chew through it with a ferocity he'd never seen.

It is said that this went on for weeks; the more work he fed the swimmers, the more their capacity for work grew. At some point, someone, perhaps Schubert himself, began to call this group of swimmers "the Animals". And the lane they trained in together became known around the nation as the Animal Lane.

Mark Schubert loved Southern California from the moment he'd arrived in 1972. The sparkling eight-lane 50-meter pool he ruled over at the Marguerite swimming complex in Mission Viejo was a world-class training facility.

Mission Viejo Coach Mark Schubert and assistant coach Selden Frischner

On a Sunday morning in April 1976, the eight lanes of blue water seemed to glow in the soft California sunlight. But there was no joy for Schubert on this radiant morning. As the swimmers filed through the chain link gate for practice, he was too preoccupied to notice the blooming bougainvillea, the nearby stand of 30-foot eucalyptus trees, or Saddleback Mountain draped with blue sky in the distance.

The pressure was mounting on his top swimmer, Shirley Babashoff, and he had a sense that she was starting to feel it. She was just weeks away from the 1976 USA Olympic Trials, and hardly a day went by without an article in the paper about Shirley and her prospects at the upcoming Montreal Olympics.

At just nineteen, Shirley was the veteran on the USA national team. She'd won two silver medals, and a gold on the 4x100-freestyle relay at the Munich Games of 1972. If she made the team, Montreal would be Shirley's second Olympics. Over the previous three years she'd done everything Schubert had asked her to do to be prepared. And yet it seemed that no amount of work could push Shirley clear of the women swimmers of the nation of East Germany.

On the pool deck, Schubert was not very tall, and he tended to stand close to the swimmers when he was talking to them out of the pool. He was a yeller at times, prone to an occasional tirade on the deck, but mostly he ruled a swim practice with an intense presence more than any actions or speech. In a practice, it seemed to the swimmers that nothing that happened across all eight lanes of the 50-meter pool escaped his notice. At a swim meet, he could project a cool demeanor, or he could fire the team up by leading a cheer before a finals session, but the one sure way to tell that Mark Schubert was excited or nervous was when he began to pull at the thick hair around the nape of his neck.

He had come from his native Ohio four years earlier, leaving behind a dead-end job and some ghosts in his past. "You might be a great coach someday," the head of the local recreation district told him after Schubert pitched the idea of enclosing one of the 50-meter pools in town, "but it won't be here in Akron." His father had wanted him to pursue a career in law, but Schubert's first swim coach, a man named Dick Wells, had so positively influenced his life that Schubert's heart was set on coaching at a young age. He idolized George Haines' coaching career at the Santa Clara Swim Club, so California became the land of Schubert's dreams.

In the four short years he'd been coaching them, his Mission Viejo swimmers had become a phenomenon even in an era that seemed to know no bounds in terms of time improvement. The Animals, Schubert's top group of athletes, was known for covering huge amounts of volume in their weekly training regimen.

He treated the boys in the Animal Lane like boys. He monitored the locker room after workouts and occasionally showed up at their homes if they were late for a morning practice— subtly implying that there was no place in their world where his influence could not reach. He loomed large and slightly threatening in their lives. Even Babashoff characterized him as a slave driver. In the first few weeks of training with Mark Schubert she admitted that he might have made her cry once or twice. [1]

With the women in his top group though, there was a subtle difference than with the boys, especially where Shirley was concerned. When she flatly refused to record daily practices in a logbook, Schubert agreed, but added, "Don't tell the other swimmers." Shorty after the '72 Games Babashoff's coach, Flip Darr, who'd helped her develop into an Olympic swimmer, temporarily retired from club coaching. She never knew the reason for Darr's abrupt departure from her swim club, but for Schubert it was something of a coup when she'd chosen Mission Viejo over several other top swim clubs within driving distance of her home.

Babashoff was the perfect icon for a new breed of elite female athlete. She was beautiful in a Southern California surfer girl way with wavy blonde hair and blue eyes reflecting the best of her Russian heritage. She was super-fit, sure of herself, and feminine with a penchant for painting her nails a rainbow of colors. At this point in her swimming career, half of the nation's top male swimmers wanted to date her, and the other half were afraid to talk to her.

Shirley Babashoff was America's best-known female swimmer of the era. *(Photo credit: Swimming World Magazine)*

After three years of phenomenal success she was America's most well-known female swimmer. In April of '76, just weeks from the world's biggest swimming competition, Shirley was more like a colleague to Schubert, partners in this effort to prepare and win in Montreal. Like any great coach, Schubert felt the burden to help her face the challenge ahead.

That challenge would come under the red, black, and gold hammer and sickle of the East German flag. No one in the international swimming community had ever seen anything like the meteoric rise of East Germany's female swimmers. In the summer of 1973 they blew past the USA women at the World Championships in Belgrade, Yugoslavia. Over the course of one swim meet, the USA had gone from the pre-eminent team in the history of international swimming to a distant second, set back on their heels and scrambling to regroup. Shirley alone had achieved some semblance of consistency in the last few years against the East Germans—and even that was sporadic.

What Schubert realized was that at this moment she could not get distracted; she definitely did not need the extra pressure of reporters asking her daily about how she thought she'd do against Kornelia Ender and the rest of the East German swimmers.

On this crisp California morning, Schubert visited with Shirley on the pool deck, standing close to her, invading her personal space in his characteristic manner while the boys started the warm-up. To survive in the Animal Lane, the swimmers learned early on that there was a time to go hard in every practice. The animals typically crawled through the first several thousand meters in anticipation of the work that lay ahead.

Typical swimming workouts in the early '70s consisted of 4,000 to 6,000 meters. But Mark Schubert took it to a new level almost immediately upon his arrival in Mission Viejo. He mostly ignored the expectations of the parent booster club who had recruited him to run a recreational level team, refusing to settle for anything less than excellence. Animal Lane workouts at certain times in the year pushed 10,000 meters in the morning and again in the evening, day after day.

Someone seeing the Animals outside of the pool, teenagers with lean bodies, bronzed skin, and sun-and-chlorine-streaked hair, might have mistaken them for a bunch of California surfers. But the tans, fit bodies, and gilded locks came from the narrow focus of countless hours spent staring at the bottom of the pool, swimming up to five hours a day and not just struggling to survive, but racing, pushing themselves to go faster and longer through each successive eleven-month training cycle.

Stories of the team's enormous volume began to leak out, and a mythology emerged around them. Over those first few years, confidence grew on the Mission Viejo club. It was unspoken, but the assumption was that when the Animals stood up to race at any meet, no one would have worked harder or longer.

The shift in the culture of elite swim training seemed in keeping with America as a whole in the turbulent 1970s. In every sphere, old boundaries were being challenged. Students protested the Vietnam War on college campuses. The civil

rights movement and women demanding equal rights dominated the television news and defined the cultural landscape.
Likewise, a revolution was taking place on the swimming
scene, and Mark Schubert's team was at the forefront.

Technological innovations meant faster and faster
swimming times. Waterproof goggles arrived at American
Swim Clubs in the fall of 1972. Form-fitting swimsuits made
of modern synthetic fabric replaced bulkier models with
skirts stretched across the thighs for modesty. And legendary
Indiana University coach and professor of physical education
Doc Counsilman's publication of *The Science of Swimming*
provided coaches a new level of technical analysis and
standardization.

The transformation of the sport in the '70s was so abrupt
that coaches and swimmers either adapted or they were
quickly left behind. Meanwhile women's collegiate swimming
in the U.S. was still in its nascent stages, with far more attention and resources—including college scholarships—devoted
to men. But the federal legislation known as Title IX was about
to change that as well. The 1976 Olympic Games in Montreal
would be the first Olympics in the post-goggle era of information and technology where the rapid changes in every area of
the sport were put to the test.

Maybe it was the memory of the women's performances at
the National Championships a few weeks earlier that was on
Schubert's mind at practice that day. Most of the USA's top
swimmers had predictably solid performances but nothing
notable, while a few new faces took the opportunity to establish themselves as contenders for a spot on the Olympic team.

Shirley had won the 200 and the 400 freestyle with times that were within striking distance of the world records.

"These swims are helping psychologically," she said after the meet, "to know I can do this well without normal shaving or tapering."[2]

Most of America's top swimmers rested from heavy training only a day or two in preparation for the Nationals. East Coast phenom Kathy Heddy, who swam under coach Frank Elm at Central Jersey Aquatics, felt the effects of training. "I'm tired," said the five-foot-four Heddy after her second-place finish to Shirley in the 400 freestyle.

In one of the few surprises of the meet, Wendy Boglioli, from Central Jersey Aquatics, broke the American Record in the 100 butterfly. Boglioli at twenty-one years of age was not a complete unknown, having won the AIAW collegiate 100 butterfly earlier in the spring in an American Record time. Another surprise came in the 100 free. Up-and-coming four-teen-year-old Jill Sterkel from El Monte Swim Club finished third—and Kim Peyton from Portland Oregon upset Shirley for the win.

For the previous five years, Peyton along with Babashoff had been a part of the USA contingent at every major international competition. Peyton's debut on the Olympic level was as an alternate on the 4x100-free relay in the morning heats in Munich, 1972. In the years between Munich and Montreal, she had become a mainstay of the USA squad. She was unique among the world-class swimmers of the day. Kim Peyton was both fun loving, a favorite of teammates and coaches, and was a fiercely strong-willed competitor.

In Oregon, she had been recognized as something of a local hero at an early age. As a seventh grader she'd gained public attention when she beat the 1968 USA Olympic Champion Debbie Meyer, who was in the last months of her career at the time. By the spring of '76, Kim at nineteen years of age had built a résumé as a go-to competitor.

Both Peyton and Babashoff were among the athletes who successfully navigated the great transition in swimming between the '72 Games and the '76 Games. In Munich Shirley was viewed as a young prodigy, fifteen years old and at the beginning of a remarkable career. Over the ensuing four years, she had become a seasoned international competitor.

As the 1976 Olympics approached, she was arguably the best female freestyle swimmer in the world. The expectations for her had grown with each spectacular season. Going into the twenty-first Olympiad, there was talk that she could come home from Montreal as famous as Mark Spitz, returning with a haul of Olympic medals that would rival his seven golds in Munich.

This was Schubert's concern. He knew his athletes. Shirley was a great competitor, but center stage—outside the pool— was not her favorite place to be. It had gotten to the point where she couldn't go to the grocery store without being recognized. More problematic, she was emerging as a superstar among USA Olympic athletes, and she was not polished in articulating her outlook on her career and her competitors to the press. She was blunt and tended to say exactly what was on her mind with no fear of how reporters might receive it.

Years after Montreal, Olympic Champion turned TV broadcaster Donna de Varona noted that unlike some athletes, her impression of Babashoff was that Shirley largely considered swimming a personal endeavor. She was one of those athletes who is both internally motivated to be her best and highly competitive in a racing environment. But at big meets where the international press was in attendance she seemed to say in a not-so-subtle way that she'd come to *swim*, not to talk to the press about *swimming*.[3] On this late spring morning, with the USA Nationals behind them and the 1976 Olympic Trials just weeks away, Babashoff swam third in the Animal Lane behind Mission Viejo native and Olympic hopeful Brian Goodell. The main set was three times 800 meters freestyle, with about a minute rest between.

The Animals had taken it particularly easy during the warm up, joking and laughing through a long kicking set. Their nonchalance did not help Mark Schubert's annoyed distraction. He could be intense and came across as angry when he felt the swimmers were not giving a workout their best efforts, but for some reason this morning he held back. Maybe he believed Shirley did not need any additional pressure to perform just then.

Now with the main set of 800 repeats underway, the Animals were all business. Behind aviator sunglasses, Schubert continuously glanced between his swimmers, his handheld stopwatch, and the huge poolside pace clock with its large sweeping second hand. The first 800 in the set of three was fast enough to have been remarkable all by itself, but if the animals were true to their training, Mark Schubert knew something special was happening.

With the second 800 underway, Schubert paced the deck pulling at his hair with his peculiar nervous habit. The Animals trained to "negative split" their races, moderating their effort on the first half then accelerating in the second half, pushing themselves to the limits of their capacity in the last half of each race. The boys swimming ahead of Shirley in the lane took the front end out fast for this 800, then stepped it up at the 400-meter mark. Babashoff cruised right behind them like a great aquatic predator tracking its prey. She thrived on competing with the boys in the Animal Lane. The second 800 was astonishing, faster than anything Schubert had seen in a practice.

Hanging on the wall with precious little rest before the final effort, muscles and lungs burning, Brian Goodell managed a raspy "Let's go" to the other Animals. Seconds later the pace clock signaled their rest was up, and the three were off, pushing toward the finish line of an unprecedented workout.

Even as the seconds ticked away, time seemed to stand still. At the halfway point, the boys were faster than they had ever been, and Shirley was just 10 seconds back. At the 700-meter turn, with 100 meters to go, Brian Goodell picked up his flutter kick and pulled away; the others straining to stay close.

At the final wall, Babashoff's time was 8 minutes and 45 seconds.

Under the California sky stretching limitless, Mark Schubert double-checked the time on his watch. He had come to expect remarkable efforts in long workouts, but this one left the coach taken aback.

"That's two seconds over the world record," he said in a way he hoped signaled some level of nonchalance, as if he saw world-record swims in practice every day.

"I wish I would have known," Shirley said, struggling to catch her breath. "I could have gone a little faster."

Mark Schubert was known among his peers as focused and driven, rarely jovial, much less cheerful. But after that extraordinary set of 800s, he might have smiled just a little. Or maybe it was just a trick of the bright California sun.

Whether he let it show, Schubert lived for these moments. He thrived on practices when athletes proved to themselves that they were capable of achieving the lofty goals they'd set. The mystique of the Animal Lane was built on the simple notion of working harder and longer than any competitors possibly would. And, at that moment, it was hard for him to imagine any training group in the world with a better work ethic.

Schubert—still in his 20s, born after the 1949 partition of Germany into "East" and "West"—had no way of knowing what ambitious coaches like himself were doing in an Eastern Bloc country across the ocean. He would do his best in the coming weeks to shield Shirley and help her focus on getting ready for the biggest meet swimming has to offer, but there was no getting around the fact that once every four years the attention of the American public was focused on the sport of swimming. And for the week of swimming at Montreal, that focus would be squarely on Shirley Babashoff, the beating heart and driving spirit of the Animal Lane. Schubert was confident in the work Shirley was doing to be ready, but he understood that for the first time in recent history, the USA women's team would go into the Olympics as underdogs.

He knew it was no time to be complacent. They'd seen it all before over the previous three years. When the USA women took a step forward, it seemed they remained two steps behind the East Germans.

Five thousand miles away, in the misty heartland of Europe, morning would dawn soon. The marvel that was the East German sport machine would awaken and resume its relentless grind toward the goal of glorifying the Communist state through sport. At state-run training sites from Leipzig to Karl Marx Stadt, Kornelia Ender, Barbara Krause, and other luminaries of swimming in East Germany were preparing just like the Animals were.

In the spring of 1976, Ender, Krause, and their East German teammates were much like Shirley and her friends, young people in the prime of their lives, striving for their own personal triumphs. They could not understand nor control the roles they'd been cast in an international drama of the Cold War era.

Chapter 2

MUNICH GAMES

AMERICAN WOMEN HAD DOMINATED Olympic swimming for decades. Starting with the first contingent of USA women swimmers at the 1920 Games in Antwerp, Belgium, with but a few challengers, the USA had been the team to beat at virtually every Olympic Games. They faced tough conditions at that first Olympics in Antwerp. The pool was a straight-shot 100-meter course with no lane dividers or markings on the bottom of the tank. Both the air and the water were cold. But in their first showing, American women swept gold, silver, and bronze in all three swimming events. By the end of the swimming competition, the USA had its very first superstar in women's swimming. Ethelda Bleib-

The USA's 4x100 Freestyle Relay of Frances Scroth, Margaret Woodbridge, Ethelda Bleibtrey and Irene Guest won the Gold Medal at the 1920 Olympics. *(Photo credit: The International Swimming Hall of Fame)*

trey emerged as a champion, winning the 100 freestyle, 300 free, and 4x100-free relay. The Americans won the relay in Antwerp with a time that was 10 seconds faster per leg than the previous Olympic record. [4]

The women were trailblazers, as athletics were still clearly a man's world. In a pattern that would continue for decades, the first women swimmers overcame hurdles not known to their male counterparts. The summer before her Olympic triumphs, Bleibtrey was arrested for "nude bathing." Apparently, she had the audacity to remove her stockings at a public swimming pool in New York City.

From Antwerp in 1920 through Munich in 1972, the USA women swimmers would win more Olympic medals than the next three countries combined. And they were particularly dominant in the 4x100-free relay, winning the event in ten of thirteen Olympic Games.

When Shirley Babashoff and her teammates arrived at the Munich Olympics in 1972, the big story, was not the USA women, but Mark Spitz and Australia's top woman swimmer, Shane Gould. In the preceding year Gould, trained by the revered Australian coach Forbes Carlisle, had achieved the unthinkable. She entered the Munich Games holding the world record in every freestyle event from the 100 to the 1,500. To date, no other swimmer has ever achieved such a feat. Even with Shane Gould's supremacy in the freestyle, the rest of the Australian team had nowhere near the depth of the USA women. While expectations ran high for Gould, across the breadth of the swimming program, everyone assumed the USA would be the team to beat.

In Munich Shirley was the new kid on the team, a rising superstar, but still only fifteen and blissfully naïve. She was giddy at the prospect of competing at the Olympics and somewhat in awe of her American Olympic teammates. When she made the team, she had to check with her mother, Vera, to make sure it was "the Olympics that are on TV." [5]

The German organizers promoted the Munich Games as the "Serene Olympics." The tranquil, muted colors of the 1972 opening ceremonies stood in stark contrast to the militaristic scenes of Adolph Hitler presiding over the Berlin Games of 1936, forever branded by the Nazi flag. The first week of the Games started off well enough. As expected, the good looks and astonishing achievements of the USA's Mark Spitz with his trademark black mustache dominated the swimming arena. On the women's side, Shane Gould performed admirably in her first and only Olympics, winning three gold, one silver and one bronze medal. Spitz won an unprecedented seven gold medals in seven world record performances.

The USA women performed well in Munich. With short, blonde swimmer hair and vivid blue eyes, Karen Moe stood atop the podium after her winning her signature event, the 200 butterfly. In the 4x100-medley relay, the backstroke leg by Melissa Belote gave the USA the lead, and they were never challenged. After Cathy Carr's breaststroke and Deanna Deardorff's butterfly legs, the race was over. Sandy

Karen Moe, 1972 Olympic Champion in the 200 Butterfly *(Photo credit: Swimming World Magazine)*

Neilson, the USA's fastest freestyler, finished her leg more than 4 seconds ahead of East Germany, which had to battle for second.

For Kim, Karen and Shirley, the 72 Olympics were a dream. They would remember the magic of the whole experience as much as the competition: the opening ceremonies, the athlete village, meeting athletes from all over the world.

Munich was the perfect setting for Babashoff's debut on swimming's largest stage. As a relative unknown, she felt no pressure to measure up to anyone's expectations but her own. As much as anything, she swam true to the training she'd grown up with under coach Flip Darr. In the 200 freestyle, she swam her distinctive back-half race with a furious charge in the last 50 meters, coming up just short of an upset of Shane Gould.

The USA won the gold medal in both relays. Shirley and her teammates barely took note of the East Germans at the meet, which wasn't surprising. Even with the East Germans entering the '72 Games as the world record holders in the 4x100-free relay, having set the mark in 1971 at the European Championships, no one considered the country a swimming power at the Munich Olympics.

The swimming competition at the Munich Games would be notable for many reasons. For starters, no one including Mark Spitz himself believed that seven gold medals in a single Games was possible. Australia's Shane Gould came into the meet with the possibility of winning five events. Even though she came away with only three gold medals, Shane single-handedly showed the world that Australia was a force to be reckoned with in women's swimming. And, though it would go almost unnoticed, Munich would be the last Olympic Games in the era before goggles were worn by swimmers in training and competition. Over the next couple of years, the tiny plastic goggle, weighing less than an ounce, was going to revolutionize swimming in a way that no piece of equipment had ever affected an Olympic sport.

In the 4x100-free relay preliminaries, the USA led off with feisty Kim Peyton, from Portland, Oregon, a fifteen-year-old fond of putting her hair up in twin pigtails. Ann Marshall, who trained with Jack Nelson in Fort Lauderdale, had the fastest split of the prelim swimmers by almost a full second.

In the finals, though, the USA coaches changed up the team and chose to lead off the relay with Sandy Nielson. Nielson entered the Olympics as the third fastest 100 freesty-ler on the USA team, and she had pulled off one of the great upsets of the Games by surging to an early lead and defeating world record holder Shane Gould. The coaches then chose the more experienced Jane Barkman, who was the only returning athlete from the USA's gold-medal winning relay four years earlier at the 1968 Olympics in Mexico City.

Nielson got the USA out front with a split only slightly slower than her individual 100 free, giving Jenny Kemp the lead by half a meter on the second leg. Kemp was slow on the exchange, and the East Germans gained slightly at the 200-meter mark. Barkman, swimming in third position, was slower than the qualifying race by a half second. With 100 meters to go, what should have been an easy win for the USA turned into one of the great races of the Games.

In the finals, both countries had chosen to swim the surprisingly reliable, yet youngest members of their squads for the anchor leg. Rising star fifteen-year-old Shirley Babashoff anchored the USA in lane 5. Next to her in lane 4 was Kornelia Ender, East Germany's thirteen-year-old prodigy. With less than 3/10 of a second separating the teams, there was no way anyone in the Munich swim stadium could know that this race would be the beginning of a four-year dual between Babashoff and Ender and that, in the interval between Munich and the Montreal, the two would become renowned as the most accomplished women swimmers of their time.

Babashoff and Ender went head-to-head twice in Munich, in the 100 freestyle and the 400-free relay. On the final leg of the relay with but a few tenths lead, Shirley misjudged her turn, barely touching the far wall with her toes. In the end, Shirley out-split

Shirley Babashoff with teammates Jenny Kemp, Sandy Nielson and Jane Barkman won the 4x100 Freestyle Relay over East Germany at the 1972 Games. *(Photo credit: Swimming World Magazine)*

Kornelia by less than 1/10 of a second. The USA needed Shirley's late surge to assure the win—by 0.21 seconds.

The USA coaches and athletes finished the week of swimming in Munich satisfied that the status quo of America's swimming superiority was pretty much intact. The USA women brought home eight of fourteen gold medals. They won five silver and four bronze. Shirley finished the competition with two silver medals and a gold in the 4x100-free relay. No one seemed to make much of the performance of the East Germans. As the swimming competition ended Shirley's clear target, it seemed, was the great Australian freestyler Shane Gould.

Perhaps the emergence of the East German women in 1972 got lost in the shadow of the dark story that came to define Munich. The "Serene Games," meant to soften the memory of a World War and a twisted Olympic spectacle from three decades prior, became the Olympics of Black September when Palestinian terrorists stormed the athlete dorms, kidnapped then murdered eleven Israeli wrestlers and coaches. Across the world, as many as 900 million viewers watched the tragedy unfold on television.

The 4x100-free relay race had taken place on Wednesday, August 30. Less than a week later, on the morning of Tuesday, September 5, the athletic achievements in the first week of the Munich Games were all but forgotten.[6] The image of an athlete village transformed into an armed camp replaced the calm images of dancers at the opening ceremonies. For millions of people around the world, the ominous hooded Palestinian smoking calmly at the doorway to the athlete dorm, not the lean mustachioed Mark Spitz, became the unforgettable image of the Munich Games.

Athletes pulled mattresses into Shirley's room in the dorms. Shane Gould and 100-freestyle champion Sandy

Nielson huddled together with the others imagining the worst. Unsure how extensive the assault on the athlete village might be, Sandy phoned home to tell her parents that she loved them. Olympic champions with bright futures ahead of them were suddenly drawn into the most infamous act of terrorism in the history of the Olympic Games.

Chapter 3

BELGRADE: THE FIRST WORLD CHAMPIONSHIPS

NO ONE WAS PREPARED for what happened at the first World Swimming Championships in Belgrade, Yugoslavia. In the twelve months between Munich and Belgrade, East Germany's women's swim team bolted from near obscurity to become the most dominant team in international swimming.

"Too much cannot be said about the supremacy of the East German team," wrote *Swimming World* editor Al Schoenfield, trying to describe the spectacle that was the East German dominance in Belgrade. "On the first day of the meet they shocked the world—seven final swims, seven world records. ..."

In the first event, Kornelia Ender and her East German teammates demolished the 400-medley relay world mark that had been set

East Germany's 4x100 Medley Relay at the First World Swimming Championships in Belgrade, Yugoslavia was anchored by Kornelia Ender [pictured on the left.] *(Photo credit: Swimming World Magazine)*

by the USA in Munich. Schoenfield recorded it this way in *Swimming World*: "[T]he four girls on the [East German] medley relay each swam under the world record. Their margin of victory over runner-up United States was so great (20 meters) that not even a wide-angle lens could register the winning margin. It was the worst defeat ever by an American relay team."[7]

Kim Peyton was described as an "electric" personality by those who knew her well.
(Photo credit: Swimming World Magazine)

While those last words must have stung a nation that had dominated international swimming, no one in the USA or elsewhere in the swimming community recognized the breadth and scope of the program that was overtaking the swimming world.

The '73 World Championships was a complete beat-down for the USA. The effect on the USA team may be best summed up by normally upbeat Kim Peyton, who along with Shirley would form the backbone of the USA women's team in the years leading up to the next Olympics in Montreal. Kim wrote home from Belgrade on Hotel Slavija stationery to tell her sisters that the hotel was a dump, she'd picked up a cold, and she was sick from drinking the water.[8]

While no one could have predicted the rapid emergence of the East Germans, the USA team was caught completely off guard. The first mistake the USA made was in approaching the inaugural World Championships as a secondary event. After the USA Nationals in Louisville, Kentucky, that summer, the top swimmers split—one squad attended the World Student Games in Moscow, the other the World Championships in Belgrade. There was no preparatory training camp for the women, and the coaching staff was made up of USA coaches with limited international experience.

More important, the women's team arrived in Belgrade without the benefit of the leadership of some of its top stars. Karen Moe, the 1972 Olympic champion in the 200 butterfly, had delayed the start of college to stay at home and train for the Munich Games. When she entered UCLA in 1972, there was no team for her to be a part of. Rumors arose of scholarships for women in the next few years, but she simply left swimming behind and focused on her kinesiology studies. Unlike the USA male swimmers who anticipated scholarships to train and compete in a robust NCAA program after high school, many of America's best women athletes from the Munich Olympics, with no options for swimming in college, simply retired at the height of their careers.

Title IX of the Educational Amendments Act that led to the funding of women's athletics in college had only been passed the previous summer. Universities were just starting to establish and fund women's programs. Women's swimming existed at an almost recreational level at a handful of universities, but no university program came near what was available for the top USA men. So while seasoned competitors led the USA men, the rising women stars were left to face the juggernaut of East Germany with less experienced leadership. This vacuum was left to be filled by Shirley and Kim.

Over the previous year, at the David Douglas club in Portland, Oregon, coach Don Jacklin had increased Kim Peyton's workload in response to what was happening at Mission Viejo with Mark Schubert's club and around the country. At some points in the season, the kids swam as many as three practices in a day. The higher volume practices worked like a charm for Kim.

In Belgrade, she was the perfect choice to go up against East Germany's world record holder, Kornelia Ender, on the first leg of the 4x100 freestyle relay. From her earliest days, Kim had found success against opponents who were supposedly unbeatable. The World Championships was Kim's third major international competition and she was starting to build confidence and experience on the international scene. But Kim's growing confidence and that of her teammates would be severely challenged in Belgrade.

The first World Championships was a coming-out party for the East Germans, and the belle of the ball was fourteen-year-old Kornelia Ender. At the beginning of the summer, the 100 freestyle world record stood at 58.5. In the weeks prior to Belgrade, Ender lowered the record twice. She swam 58.2 in July and 58.1 in August.

In drab, unfriendly Belgrade, a little under the weather and none too impressed with Yugoslavia, Kim managed a 59.0 lead-off leg—a time that was among the best in the world. Even so, Ender scorched the first 50 meters, leaving Kim Peyton and the rest of the field to race for second. Kim, who'd swum just over a minute in the previous summer in Munich, scrambled just to stay in contact. Kathy Heddy, swimming second for the USA, dove in almost a second and a half behind Ender's new world record of 57.61. At that point in the history of the sport, no other woman had ever swum under 58 seconds.

The results in Belgrade were devastating. The USA 4x100-free relay of Kim Peyton, Kathy Heddy, Heather Greenwood, and Shirley Babashoff saw the East Germans win the relay by more than 3 seconds—an eternity in a swim race. By the end of the meet, Kim wanted no more of Yugoslavia. She was ready to come home. "Americans are very much hated in Yugoslavia," she wrote to her sisters before returning to her genuinely plucky personality.

In addition to Kim's general malaise, Shirley, America's rising superstar, came out flat. She was at the far end of a summer season that had reached its pinnacle at the National Championships two weeks earlier. In the 100 freestyle, Shirley tied to the hundredth of a second with Enith Brigitha of Holland, both girls finishing behind Ender by more than a second. In the 200 freestyle Shirley was beaten at her own game. She went out a little faster than she had at the Nationals, only to be run down from behind by teammate Keena Rothhammer. Americans Heather Greenwood and Rothhammer finished first and second in the 400 free. The only other event won by an American was Melissa Belotte's win in the 200 backstroke. After that, it was all East Germany.

The USA team could do little but watch the East German

onslaught of the record book. The end result was the biggest rout of an American team in the history of the sport. East German swimmers, who just twelve months earlier at Munich came away with four silver and one bronze medals, won ten of fourteen events.

After the stunning display of the East Germans on the first day of competition at Belgrade, where they won all seven events in world record time, the only area the rest of the world found consistent success against the East Germans was in the distance events.

Almost immediately questions began to be asked, and suspicions raised. *Swimming World* ran an article entitled, "Why are the East Germans so Good?" on the same page as the World Championship summary. The magazine also translated an article from a French newspaper where a defector from East Germany laid out allegations of steroid use. Whispers of "elixirs against fatigue" and male hormone use began to surface. For their part, if they did respond, officials and coaches from East Germany pointed to the comprehensive nature of their training system and early selection of children to track as potential world-class athletes. [9] Mostly, the East German coaches and administrators were simply silent on the allegations.

The swimming community suspected doping right away, but without proof, no one was willing to cry foul, and the very nature of the closed society in East Germany leant itself perfectly to airtight secrecy.

Adding to the confusion of the bewildering results, the

Belgrade World Championships marked the advent of an entirely new swimsuit design for women. Shirley, Kim, and their teammates had come to the starting blocks in old style, loose fitting nylon suits with a vertical stars and stripes pattern. Kornelia Ender and her teammates came to the blocks in a high-necked blue suit made of "ribolastic" that fit tightly to every curve of the body.

It became known as the "Belgrade Suit," and it was distinctive for two major features. First, the suit was more form fitting, to the point that the immediate reaction of most of the USA women was regarding the propriety of the suit. The second feature that raised eyebrows was the lack of the skirt at the crotch. The requirement for this tiny piece of fabric, presumably for modesty, had been dropped by FINA, the international governing body for swimming. As coaches, athletes, and journalists scrambled for answers to the East Germans' overnight ascendancy, some pointed to the new suit.

As radical as the suit was for the time, it was a far cry from tech-suit fabrics and design of the decades to come. Nonetheless, Al Schoenfield and the writers of *Swimming World* would soon coin the phrase "suit wars" to describe the competition between major swimsuit manufacturers in their efforts to release the next must-have suit of each successive year. In truth, every modern-day wonder suit of the twenty-first century can trace its roots to Belgrade in 1973.

The "supremacy of the East German team," as Al Schoenfield described it, was so sudden and complete that observers of the revolution in Belgrade had no reference for what they were seeing. [10] As for Shirley, Kim and their young teammates,

Belgrade marked a crossroads. American women swimmers could either acquiesce to the German swim machine, or they could go home and redouble their efforts in anticipation of the next meeting and the long march toward the 1976 Olympics in Montreal.

While the personnel of the USA and East German teams would change some at the major championships in the lead-up to Montreal, Belgrade began a three-year battle. And the East Germans took the early advantage.

Chapter 4

THE MAKING OF A CRUSADER

VISITORS TO EAST GERMANY during the '50s and '60s
likened the experience to stepping into a black-and-white film
from yesteryear. The country had been bombed into submis-
sion by the Allies in the months leading to the end of World
War II, and for decades after the war, surreal landscapes of
rubble remained where buildings and factories once stood.

A proud people, Germany found itself a pariah among the
nations after the war. Adolph Hitler's Nazi aggression had led
to the death of 55 million people worldwide. Of that number,
more than half were Soviets. [11] After Germany's unconditional surrender in May of 1945, political edict at the global level
effectively divided the nation between the Allies. Communist
Russia took over administration of East Germany while the
USA, Britain, and France oversaw post-war reconstruction
and nation-building in West Germany.

When Germany split, real people were left to piece together
lives and families as two new German nations emerged. In the
East, the Russians were ruthless in their establishment of a
Communist regime. Early on, people were arrested under the
pretense of purging any remnant of the previous Nazi regime
or because of anti-Communist sentiments. Many times these
actions spiraled into a characteristic lawlessness. It would take

five years for the Communist Party to consolidate its rule. And it would take another two decades before the United Nations would recognize East Germany as a sovereign state. [12]

Even as the chaos subsided and the newly formed nation adjusted to the hegemony of the Soviet Union, sport was emerging as a means of establishing East German identity. Sport was an easy, relatively inexpensive, and nonthreatening (to mother Russia) way to gain positive exposure on the international stage.

It's tenuous to draw analogies between the 1936 Berlin Olympics when the Nazi Party sought to demonstrate the superiority of the Aryan race and the East German desire to gain some semblance of national pride through international sport. But as early as 1952, facing the enormous cost of post-war reconstruction, the East German leadership, following a program known as State Planning Theme 14.25 determined to promote sport, constructing 122 sport stadiums, more than 1,100 large indoor field houses, and 47 indoor swimming pools. [13]

The East German constitution went so far as to assert in one of its articles that "physical culture, sport and outdoor pursuits promote, as elements of socialist culture, the all-around physical and mental development of the individual."

One of the young people who benefitted from the investment in sport was Brigitte Berendonk. In the summer of 1958, as the junior champion in heptathlon, she was being considered for inclusion in one of East Germany's elite sport schools. As a rising star in the state-run track program, a bright future lay ahead for this pre-teen. But her young life was about to

Brigitte Berendonk became an Olympian for West Germany after her family escaped East Germany. *(Photo credit: Brigitte Berendonk courtesy of USA Swimming)*

take an abrupt turn that would eventually lead back to a full intersection with the surprising rise of East Germany's women swimmers.

Faced with the mandates of the socialist command economy, the future for the four Berendonk children was both known and a bit of a mystery. By edict, each would be relegated to career paths that met the needs of the nation, as determined by the government. Brigitte's father was a medical doctor, and the children were bright. They learned music in the home and were voracious readers. Under the East German system, only one might be allowed to follow in their father's footsteps and study medicine. Of the remaining kids, if it was decided that the State needed bricklayers, Brigitte's brothers might become bricklayers. She and her sisters might be directed toward university training to become schoolteachers, or they might work in a factory or on a large state-run wheat farm. In the end, the State would decide with little input from the Berendonks.

Before the construction of the Berlin Wall in 1961, each year as many as 200,000 East Germans made their way from the East to live permanently in the West. Of that number it is estimated that half were under the age of twenty-five. [14] Before the Wall, leaving the country for a visit to West Berlin was allowed, but leaving the country with the intent of starting a new life in the West was a crime, punishable by imprisonment.

The Berendonk family discussed the possibility of leaving East Germany, but only at home. Speaking up about East Germany's economy or political system, even with the simplest question, such as why the West had more and better automobiles, was cause for discipline at school. The Berendonk parents told their kids to keep their opinions to themselves. In the end, as much as the absence of choice in their future, the reality that asking the wrong question could lead to discipline and suspicion became reason enough for the family to make a decision. So around Christmastime in 1958 the Berendonk family made the daring choice to join the most costly East German exodus of human industry, creativity, and potential.

The Berendonks organized their escape plan quietly around the kitchen table. For the children, it was both exciting and unnerving to leave for a life of unknowns in the West. They would travel in pairs. Each pair had a story. Brigitte's story was that her parents had given her this trip to Berlin as a reward for winning the East German heptathlon championship. As with any good lie, it held some truth.

"My parents were not that type of parents," she remembers with a smile. "It was a very good story, but they would never have given any of us kids such a reward." [15]

Standing on the subway platform in the winter of 1958 with her brother, she would have been hard to picture as a future world-class athlete. Much in need of strength training, she was thin with short-cropped dark hair and glasses. Ironically, she was the only one of the family with any reservations about leaving East Germany. The selection into one of the sport schools was a prestigious honor she was reluctant to give up.

The Berendonk kids carried nothing other than what a normal citizen on a day trip would carry. If East German officials questioned them at the border, they were simply on a day-long holiday to see the sights in West Germany. But at the moment of truth, the crossing from East to West became no drama at all. Brigitte and her brother simply boarded the subway in East Germany, paid the minimal subway toll, rode for three stops and exited into West Germany.

If Westerners visiting the East were struck by the draining of color from the world, Brigitte and her siblings must have felt like they'd emerged from the subway into a Technicolor movie. Indeed, one of their first experiences in the West was two epic Hollywood films. With money their grandmother cobbled together, the kids saw *Gone With the Wind* and *The Bridge on the River Kwai* on the big screen in downtown Berlin. Their expectations of the world began to change in ways they could scarcely imagine.

While Brigitte may have felt uncertain about her future, without knowing it, her parents' decision to seek a better life for their children had saved Brigitte from almost certain inclusion in what has been described as the sporting crime of the twentieth century: the mass doping of East German Olympic athletes.

Years later, this girl, as a grown woman, would become a West German Olympic athlete and later emerge as the prime crusader against the doping program of the East German sport system. Decades later she would take up the fight against the abuses that took place against young athletes on the campuses of the very state-run institutions she'd longed to be a part of.

The political and cultural dynamics that led to East Germany's state-sponsored doping program are impossible to untangle from the history of Germany in the aftermath of the Second World War. Out of the confluence of history, culture, and perhaps as much as any factor, a failing economy, the leaders of the nation determined to express national prominence on the stage of international athletics. And at some point, the East German Olympic Committee, the ruling governmental authority for sport, and a cadre of medical doctors, scientists, and coaches began to experiment with the use of steroids as a means of achieving the goal of athletic superiority.

The seasoned international coaching community did not have any idea that they were looking at steroid-enhanced performances when they watched Kornelia Ender and her teammates in their sleek Belgrade "skin suits" at the first World Championships. Decades later the world of international sport would come to call this category of drugs performance enhancing drugs, or PEDs. Far from being an anomaly in 1973, PEDs were already a well-established means of gaining an unfair advantage in other sports. USA weightlifters were among the first and most egregious abusers of anabolics. But in swimming up to this point, doping was all but unknown. From the Belgrade championships until the fall of the Berlin Wall in 1989, steroid abuse administered by East German doctors and coaches would be a scourge on international swimming.

Many athletes from the doping era are quick to recognize the little blue pill that was part of the daily cocktail their coaches described to them as "vitamins." The pill, now known to be Oral Turinabol, an anabolic steroid manufactured by state-run pharmaceutical company VEB Jenapharm, was only available in East Germany.

While it is clear that some level of doping in swimming must have been in effect in the months prior to the Belgrade World Championships, Ines Geipel, chairman of the German support group for victims of the doping program, refers to 1974 as the starting point of universal steroid doping. [16] Anti-doping crusaders Brigitte Berendonk and her husband, Dr. Werner Franke, believe the doping program in its very earliest and crudest stages began in July 1968.

Franke, a world-renowned microbiologist and cancer researcher, met Berendonk in their youth when Franke, a mediocre middle-distance runner, boldly offered to coach young Brigitte in her discus throw. As young track and field competitors, they had established friendships and numerous colleagues among the East German coaches and athletes before the Berlin Wall effectively sealed off East Germany from prying eyes. Their vantage point as observers of the East German sport world at the inception of the doping program gave them unique insight into the early effects of male hormones administered to young women.

For Franke and Berendonk, the situation was untenable. According to their best observations, the first East German doping subject was a woman shot putter, a former competitor of Brigitte's. In an original East German report coded 1/68, the twenty-seven-year-old woman was put on drugs beginning July 28, 1968. In just three months of anabolic steroid doping, this early experiment yielded an improvement of 2 meters, a world record, and a gold medal at the 1968 Olympics in Mexico City. [17]

In any case, by the time of the 1976 Montreal Games, the doping program was in high gear. And for whatever reason the East German women swimmers were among those who saw the most performance enhancement from anabolics. In a post-Montreal memo to the East German secret police, or STASI, one of the architects of the doping program, Dr. Manfred Hoppner, set out the vision for the future of women's swimming in East Germany in stunningly cavalier language.

"Anabolics are used in all Olympic sports, and the effects of the performances are undoubted. Remarkable rates of performance enhancement with women swimmers, this is where our greatest strength and advantages are."

Hoppner, a physician and well-respected scientist outside of East Germany, became such a key player in maintaining

Innovation was everywhere, but without a doubt California was the hotbed of competitive swimming. From north to south, California swim programs set the standard for Olympic swimming worldwide. Australians, Canadians, and eventually the East Germans studied and emulated the USA, and they focused most intently on what was happening in the Golden State.

At this point in the history of the sport, no one had more experience coaching at the highest level than George Haines. Before there was Mission Viejo, there was Haines' Santa Clara Swim Club. More than any other swim program in the world, what coach George Haines began in 1957 still shines as one of the great dynasties in USA Olympic sport. Entering the Dallas National Championships in the spring of 1974, Haines and his squad were seeking their fortieth championship title. Almost every well-known swimmer of the 1960s was a product of Haines and his program: Don Schollander, Donna de Varona, Claudia Kolb, swimmers whose accomplishments made them close to household names all had ties to the program. Karen Moe went from promising age grouper to Olympic champion under Haines' guidance.

The interchange of ideas and information between coaches was perhaps unique among highly developed Olympic sports. In his first summer coaching at Mission Viejo, Mark Schubert spent time visiting Jim Montrella's Lakewood Swim Club. He also observed George Haines at Santa Clara, and coach Sherm Chavoor, who was known for producing great distance swimmers.

Coaches of the era were open to new ideas. The American

entrepreneurial spirit of coaching fueled by access to information helped push the sport forward. Coaches were creative. Montrella painted the lines on the bottom of the pool at his first job coaching at the San Pedro YMCA and recruited local kids from the free swim hours to start his first team.

As age-group swimming evolved from summer club swimming to year-round programs with professional coaches, the talent pool expanded, as did the information and technology relating to competitive swimming. But it may be that a simple, practical decision by Mark Schubert coupled with the tiniest, most revolutionary piece of training equipment were the catalyst for this super era of swimming.

The idea was simple in Schubert's mind. Upon his arrival in 1972 at Mission Viejo, before Shirley Babashoff or any other world-class athletes joined the team, Schubert studied the National Time Standards and determined that the easiest event his swimmers could get a national qualifying time in was the mile. Immediately he began to push his swimmers' daily training volume. But without the invention of the simple plastic swim goggle, Mission Viejo's legendary training would not have been possible.

Coaches and swimmers remember goggles first appearing on the pool deck at the National Championships in Hershey, Pennsylvania, 1972. Coach Don Sonia became known as "the goggle man." Sonia would walk the pool deck with blue, purple, red, clear, and smoke-black goggles all up and down his arms, like a walking goggle kiosk, whipping them off his arm with a flourish upon each sale.[21]

Essential goggle design has changed little since those that appeared at the Hershey Nationals. And it is hard to understand why it took so long for the design to reach the mainstream. For decades competitive swimmers had struggled to protect their eyes and improve underwater vision with a variety of mask-like creations, taken in essence from scuba mask designs.

Prior to the goggle, swimmers came home with bright red eyes from the irritation of chlorine. At night, residual water coated the eyes making rainbow circles around every set of oncoming car lights. Swimmers at the dawn of the goggle era remember the immediacy of the revolution. Coaches brought home large plastic bags of goggles from the '72 American Swim Coaches World clinic. On Monday no one would wear them. By Friday, no one would practice without them.

Practically speaking, coaches who typically held hour-long practices of 3,000 yards were suddenly able to hold practice sessions of 5,000, 6,000, or 8,000 yards. Kids who were accustomed to swimming an hour for practice before goggles, found themselves in the pool for two to three hours.

In '72, the building wave of information, ever-increasing hours of training in the pool and the humble swim goggle unleashed an unprecedented statistical anomaly just two years later. Even the great George Haines could not have been prepared for what happened at the Dallas Nationals.

The rush for the latest suit technology turned comical at Dallas. Don LaMont's El Monte team could only get their hands on one of the Belgrade suits, so the girls passed it around between events. Even so, the AAU, which oversaw swimming rules in the USA at the time, was a year behind FINA in adopting the no-skirt policy for women's suits. LaMont, who was raising his next group of stars after the retirement of 1972 100 freestyle Olympic Champion Sandy Nielson, sat in the stands while a team mom frantically tried to sew a strip of cloth on the Belgrade suit so it would comply with the AAU "skirt" rule.

The Dallas meet made a great impression on fourteen-year-old Jill Sterkel. In a talk to swim coaches, Don LaMont had described her a year earlier as a kid "who ate weights for breakfast." She was star-struck at the prospect of competing in the same meet with Shirley Babashoff, her idol in swimming. With the Belgrade suit, high-volume sprint training, and weight training under Don LaMont's guidance, Jill dropped

her time in the 100 free by more than a second in Dallas. Buried deep in the early heats, Jill's 53.79 was well off qualifying for a swim in the finals, but the trajectory of her rapid improvement was sustained and propelled forward at the meet.

Jill Sterkel's international swimming career spanned more than a decade. *(Photo credit: Swimming World Magazine)*

Whether great swimmers are born with natural motor-skill genius in their DNA is doubtful. The records show that very few of the nation's best ten-year-old swimmers ever become Olympians. El Monte's Jill Sterkel is an exception to that rule. She qualified for her first National Championship at age eleven. More typically, the young kids who become world-class swimmers are the ones who catch the fever. At some point, out of desperation, trying to keep up with those more talented ten-year-olds, the future greats commit themselves to cracking the code, figuring out the art of capturing and maintaining pressure on the elusive hydrogen-and-oxygen compound that makes up a water molecule.

On a running track, athletes accelerate most simply by applying more pressure to the stationary point at which their shoe is in contact with the ground. But applying more power in swimming does not necessarily yield more velocity. Any college linebacker down at the pool racing his swim team buddy will attest to the fact that more strength does not in itself yield more speed. What yields more speed is repetition and attention to detail that borders on obsession. Something called focused practice—and lots of it.

The acceleration of swim speed among the USA's top women pushed everyone beyond limits previously known. In New Jersey, Wendy Boglioli noticed that her coach Bill Palmer stood next to lane one. So she made it her goal to get faster, compete with the boys in the pool, and eventually move toward the lane where Palmer seemed to pay the most attention. In Oregon, Kim Peyton trained more like a distance swimmer than a 100 freestyle sprinter. Her stroke was questionable at times, but it got the job done. Shirley Babashoff was lucky. She was surrounded by ambitious future Olympians at Mission Viejo.

Just up the California 5 Freeway, Jill Sterkel was equally fortunate. The El Monte Swim Team had become known for producing great freestyle sprinters.

Jill was a reasonably good swimmer early on, but her progress at El Monte was astounding. She came to competitive swimming like many of the USA's best swimmers still do, by way of the learn-to-swim program at the community pool near her home in Hacienda Heights. From there, she joined the recreational team where summer-club duals and a city championship were the big meets.

Jill's mom, Joanne, a former distance freestyle swimmer with the LA Aquatics club, believed she saw something special in her daughter. So Joanne had moved Jill to the El Monte Swim Club at the age of ten. The club was by no means the largest in the Southern California swimming scene, but Don LaMont had earned the reputation of developing swimmers with a view toward their long-term success.

It turns out that LaMont, by emphasizing in-water power and weight training, was a man ahead of his time. And Jill Sterkel was a perfect fit for his program. She may have eaten weights for breakfast, but what set her apart in LaMont's memory was the internal drive of a great competitor.

When young Jill Sterkel walked into the team room at El Monte for the first time she saw two sayings in large lettering on the wall that laid out the vision and philosophy for her success:

"The dictionary is the only place where success comes before work." - and - "If you're going to swim fast, you have to swim fast."

So Jill cut her teeth on the simple value of hard work. As a tenacious ten-year-old sitting on the bench with the other kids in her heat, entry card in hand, she had but one goal: break 60 seconds in the 100 freestyle. In the final meet of that summer season, she met her goal.

For Kim Peyton, Wendy Boglioli, and Shirley Babashoff the experience was the same. The direct correlation between focused hard training and personal success was the clarifying lesson of competitive swimming.

At those historic 1974 Nationals, Mark Schubert's team finished second as Haines won his historic fortieth national team title. But the revolution had begun. Mark Schubert went from a whiz-kid coach known mostly for fast butterfly swimmers to the symbol of what it meant to succeed in the new world where big training volume shifted the known paradigm. The super-era of high volume and dramatic time drops would define world-class swim training for decades.

Dallas also gave hope that while the East Germans were pulling ahead, the USA women were breaking down barriers of their own.

Chapter 6

THE DUAL MEET

IN AUGUST 1974, the East Germans came to Concord, California, for a dual meet with the USA. The leaders of the East German swim program had determined from the outset that their women would need to face the Americans with some regularity if for no other reason than to take some of the mystique away from the USA team.

The USA used the Concord Long-Course National Championship Meet to select an all-star team that would face the East Germans. The Concord meet, like Dallas, had been characterized by the continued acceleration of times in every event.

"I lowered my time by four seconds, but moved down on the U.S. Best Times lists," said one of America's best swimmers after the Concord Nationals. [22]

At the mid-point between Munich and Montreal, the marketing genius of holding the summer National Championships in Northern California followed by a dual meet that pitted the USA against the East Germans one week later helped fuel the popularity of the sport nationally and maintained the momentum Mark Spitz had generated. Many of the young swimmers who'd competed at the Nationals stayed in Northern California an extra week in order to watch the event which came to be known as "The Dual Meet of the Century." [23]

The East Germans arrived in Northern California after almost eighteen hours of travel. In the Haight-Ashbury district of San Fransisco and on the streets around UC Berkeley, Kornelia Ender and her teammates must have felt like they had landed on a different planet.

The Germans lived in a nation ruled by propaganda constructions such as "The Party is Always Right" [24], while American TV sets were exploding with news reports of President Richard Nixon's resignation stemming from the break-in of his political rivals' offices at the Watergate Hotel. The nation of East Germany, determinedly utilitarian in its architecture and staunchly proletariat in its politics, could not have been a more stark contrast to the USA in 1974.

Northern California was home to George Haines' legendary Santa Clara Swim Club, so fans were well versed in international swimming. For the 1974 USA vs. East Germany dual meet, the swimming community came out in unprecedented numbers on two perfect California evenings. The first evening of the dual was cool and clear in the arid, rolling hills of the East Bay. Fans filled temporary bleachers beyond capacity.

The East German women showed up with plenty of momentum from the European Championships in Vienna, Austria, where they set nine world records. Even so, the dual meet scoring combined the men's and women's team scores, which clearly favored the USA because the East German men were no match for the American men swimmers.

For the USA coaches, one key strategy was to quickly establish esprit de corps between the men's and women's teams.

The California press picked the women as the underdogs, so the men's team gave an overwhelming show of support to the women's team from the outset. The USA women and men stood and cheered together throughout the two-day event. The meet was unlike anything seen in international swimming with just four competitors, two from each country, racing one another in the middle lanes of the pool.

The Concord Dual Meet also saw the emergence of coach Jack Nelson, a man whom swimmers would describe as a ball of energy with a perpetual smile. This was his first major international competition as the USA women's head coach. Later that fall, Nelson would be named head coach for the 1976 women's team at Montreal.

At age 44, Nelson was an established young coach whose Fort Lauderdale Swim Team boasted some of the USA's top sprinters. A gregarious man originally from Waycross, Georgia, with a flair for self-promotion, Nelson became well loved as mentor to dozens of young coaches. Over a decades-long

Jack Nelson at the International Swimming Hall of Fame pool in Ft. Lauderdale, FL. *(Photo credit: The International Swimming Hall of Fame)*

career, he was also known as a pioneer in practical sports psychology. Back home in Florida, emblazoned on everything from plastic cups to T-shirts and beach towels was Nelson's famous Fort Lauderdale Area Swim Team tagline, "Access to Success is Through the Mind." At the Concord dual meet with the support of the USA men's team and both Kim Peyton and Shirley Babashoff swimming well, the USA women easily accepted Nelson's message of positivity.

He told *Swimming World*, "The girls got together and decided that whatever they swam, they were to try to split the East German girls all the way down if possible," meaning if the East Germans took first in an event, the USA girls would try to get second in order to prevent a sweep. [25]

On the first evening of the meet, in response to coach Nelson's public declaration, Shirley and Kim swam to a 1-3 finish in the 200 freestyle. The girls were on their game. During this two-week period in Concord, Shirley began to assert herself as one of the world's best distance swimmers. At the Nationals a week earlier she'd set the world record in the 400 freestyle. At the dual meet, she won the 400 free and finished second to American Jo Harshbarger in the 800 in a 1-2 sweep of the Germans.

Then Kim finished second to Kornelia Ender in the 100 free on day two of the meet, lowering her American Record for the third time in a week. Among the emerging stars for the USA was fifteen-year-old Kathy Heddy, who had made her international debut the previous summer in Belgrade. Kathy was something of the East Coast's answer to Shirley. Kathy was tiny to the point that, when they lined up on the starting blocks, the East German women towered over her.

At the dual meet Kathy competed in an amazing range of events: the 200 breaststroke and 4x100-free relay on day one; on day two she swam the 100 free and the 200 IM in back-to-back events, setting an American record in the IM.

A year after their anemic effort in Belgrade and feeling the energy of the hometown crowd, the USA relay swimmers were on a roll. Kathy led off the 4x100-free relay splitting more than a second faster than Ender, who fell behind after misjudging the turn. Kathy lowered Kim's American Record. In the second match-up since the East German win in Belgrade, the USA team of Kathy, Kim, Shirley, and Jill Sterkel's teammate, El Monte's Ann Marshall, reclaimed the world record in the 4x100-free relay.

With overflow crowds and the biggest press corps in attendance at a swim meet since the Munich Games, Nelson's natural showmanship came out. At five-foot four-inches Jack Nelson stood a little less than eye to eye with most of the women on the team, but he moved through a crowd much larger. He was square-jawed and loud. He smiled constantly, seemed to know everyone on the pool deck, and shook everyone's hand. In his role as spokesperson, Nelson was comfortable with the press, and he crafted his message in a folksy North Georgia way.

"Naturally, we're fantastically pleased with the women's performance," he told the press. "The East German girls are great. And the American girls can stand up to a challenge. That's why they're great." [26]

The USA behind solid performances from Kim, Shirley,

and Kathy, took a step toward keeping the American team at least within sight of the East Germans.

The dual meet was the first time anyone in the USA, apart from a handful of coaches and swimmers, had seen the East German women's team up close. The average height and weight of the women on both teams might have been the first clue that the playing field was tilted in favor of the Germans. In fact, the East German women competing in Concord were on average two inches taller and about 20 pounds heavier than the American swimmers. [27]

Among those in the stands at Concord, watching with interest as East Germany's swimmers passed by, was '72 Olympic Champion Karen Moe. In a few weeks she would return for her junior year of college and resurrect her swimming career as a member of the newly organized women's team at UCLA. But she was hesitant at anything beyond a comeback aimed at collegiate swimming. She'd learned early on from her mother and father to speak truthfully and was among the first women to speak up about what the press would mostly ignore over the next decade.

"It was one thing to read about or see a photo of the East German women, but quite another to see them in their 'skin suits,' racing in Northern California. I was in my second year at UCLA, caught up in the joy of learning at the time," Karen said. "I loved kinesiology and saw everything through the eye of a student. I went to the USA vs. East Germany dual to see some friends and watch the meet. As a young scientist, a student of human performance, I knew as soon as I saw them that something was not right with the East Germans." [28]

In some of the pictures from those early years of the doping program, before the East German doctors and coaches began to perfect dosages, the women appear with unnatural, bulging biceps and forearms, like twisted balloon art creations.

"I remember talking with the press at some point and saying I did not want to participate in a sport where the athlete with the best chemist wins," Karen said. "It was circumstantial, not evidential, at that point, but it was clear to me that they were using performance enhancing drugs. They were heavier than all of the American girls and they were super lean."

Years later, Karen Moe would characterize the struggle of the next decade and a half not as one of political ideologies, fueled by anabolic steroids, but simply a battle of good versus evil. The natural will and preparation of an athlete versus the unnatural. Success enhanced by chemistry. Clean sport versus cheating.

The doping program somehow hoodwinked the top coaches at least initially. After the East Germans and the USA, the Canadians, under the guidance of Cecil Colwin, were emerging as a major power in international swimming. The Canadians had been at the Concord Nationals in force with more than fifty of their best swimmers because Colwin, the architect of Canadian team preparations for Montreal, sought to toughen the team with competition at the highest level. At the Nationals the week prior to the dual meet, Canadian Wendy Cook led the way for her country, winning the 200 backstroke with the second fastest time in the world. The Canadians had hired expert coaches and invested heavily in facilities in hopes that its swim team, among the best of its Olympic Sport contingents, would win some medals for the host nation in 1976.

Cecil Colwin was a man with extensive international experience. He had coached many of South Africa's Olympians from the pool at his home. When South Africa was banned from Olympic competition because of apartheid, he immigrated to Australia. In '73 the Canadians hired him as technical director for all of Canadian Swimming to mastermind the trajectory of team preparations for the Montreal Games.

Colwin had seen it all over decades of international coaching. So it is hard to understand how a man of his experience could have missed the clues of steroid use in the East Germans. At Concord, he spent hours with the East German team, interviewing coaches and officials both formally and informally. Everyone it seems was looking for an answer as to the dominance of the East Germans.

In striking contrast to Karen Moe's assessment, Colwin initially described the East Germans as simply "taller and heavier than the American girls."[29] The fact is that Colwin had not seen it all. In fact no one anywhere in the world, in any sport, had ever encountered an entire athletic squad of steroid-enhanced women athletes. So began a pattern in the international swimming community that would continue for fifteen years.

It wasn't until the fall of the Berlin Wall in 1989 that the scope of East Germany's national conspiracy became known. At Concord, barely a year into the systematic doping program, coaches and swimmers in the USA and other western nations were caught in a real dilemma. Like Cecil Colwin, the swimming community outside of the Communist Bloc countries was unwilling to make unfounded accusations of steroid use. Colwin was a scientist by trade and one of the big thinkers in the sport; late in his career he would connect the principles of fluid dynamics and stroke technique. Though he might have been as wise as a serpent, he evidently did not recognize the brood of vipers who were lying to him during his observations at Concord. In the end, he simply took the East German coaches and officials at their word.

"What we saw at Concord could be described as a synthesis of the East German approach to sport and swimming in particular—good organization and intelligent implementation," Colwin said.

After a week with the team, Colwin became enamored with the notion of a systematic "intelligent" approach to national team development, essentially calling out to the skeptics to stop whining and embrace modern methods: "Good psychology, medical assistance, nutritional knowledge … [T]hese are all areas available to any coach or nation willing to take the preparation of athletes out of the normal framework.

"The administrators of the sport in [East Germany] have been efficient ('grundlich') and have taken great care to explore all the areas that could prove practical in developing their standards." [30]

Without definitive evidence of steroid use, what else did anyone outside of East Germany really have to go on? Wide scale doping of women athletes was unheard of. The rest of the world, like Cecil Colwin, was left to conclude that the astounding rise of the women swimmers must have been attributable to the combination of factors within the East German "system."

If Colwin had known the consequences his Canadian national team would face in the final results at the Montreal Games, the eminent coach would likely not have been as quick to assume that fair play meant the same thing to East Germany as it meant to him and his colleagues in the West.

Chapter 7

THE WALL

NO ONE CAN SAY FOR SURE when the widespread doping of East German athletes began. Ines Geipel, the chairman of The Doping Opfer Hilfe (DOH), translated Doping Victims Assistance Organization, refers to 1974 as the beginning of government sponsored doping. Whether State Planning Theme 14.25 morphed into steroids in 1968, 1973, or 1974 is of little consequence. In women's swimming, doping began sometime before the first World Swimming Championships in the summer of 1973.

A writer by trade, Geipel speaks thoughtfully, words full of weight, of the generation of young athletes who were subjected to steroid doping during the East German dictatorship of Erich Honecker:

"A state plan was formulated," she says, "and 12,000 to 15,000 children—youths, young talent—were included in it. It was a big chemical experiment.

Ines Geipel Director of the support group for former East Geman athletes who were doped by their coaches and team doctors *(Photo credit: USA Swimming)*

"It was … the generation that grew up in the '60s, after the construction of the [Berlin] Wall. These are the ones who were brought into this program. Their motivation to get into sport was they had talent and they wanted to see the world." [31]

Ines Geipel herself was among the world's most elite track athletes and subject to daily doses of Oral Turinabol. At the European Championships in 1980, she and three teammates set a new world record in the 4x100 sprint relay.

Today she lives in a stylish apartment with high ceilings, full of light, on a block just inside what was once the western zone of Berlin. She spends much of her time wrestling with the implications of the period before German unification and running the DOH, which grew out of the Berlin doping trials held a decade after German reunification.

"The history of East Germany has still not been told. We know a little bit about the structure because we have the STASI documents. But the history of the athletes, we learn a little bit more every day. The last half year alone, (2014) 500 more of those affected—who have talked about the worst damages done to them—have come forward." [32]

As a rising teenage track star, Ines Geipel was like the other athletes in Eastern Bloc countries. She wanted to see the world. In this way, the women athletes of East Germany were no different than their American competitors. Shirley, Jill, Kim, and others on the USA team marveled at the unique travel opportunities that international swimming competitions provided them.

Kim and Shirley's first international trip, ironically, was as part of the first USA vs. East Germany dual meet in 1971. By all accounts, '71 was well before the wholesale doping of the East German swimmers, so the USA won the dual meet easily. For Shirley and Kim that was the beginning of international swimming careers that would see the two become the most experienced competitors on the USA team in the ensuing years.

For Geipel and the other East German athletes, the culture they were growing up in could not have been more different from that of their American counterparts. On an August night in 1961, the nation of East Germany, in one of the most outrageous attempts to control a population, began construction of the Berlin Wall. From then on, ordinary citizens were simply not allowed to leave the country freely.

Elite athletes like Kornelia Ender and Ines Geipel were the exception. The leaders of Erich Honecker's Communist regime regarded their world-class athletes as a means of promoting the prestige of the nation in the international community. Honecker referred to them as "ambassadors in tracksuits." Post-unification East Germans like Ines Geipel see it in darker terms—citizens of East Germany were a commodity to be exploited for their value to the State.

"If someone is thirteen to fourteen years old and loves to swim or loves to play soccer, that's the most beautiful thing there is. Then a society [East Germany] grabs that and kills it. We lived in a time of civilian sports soldiers," Geipel says.[33]

In the '70s the cultural and personal pressure on East German athletes was incredible. East German swimmers were careful to maintain their status as world-class athletes for fear of losing access to the most common, everyday items enjoyed in the West.

"This isn't just a story about statistics and medals and standings in the Olympic Games," observes sports historian Andrew Strenk. "There are real people involved here."

Strenk, a former lecturer at USC who swam for the USA on the 1968 Olympic team, was fluent in German, so he befriended the East Germans and, by a number of coincidences, came to know some of the swimmers and doctors on a personal level. "It's important to know how the East German system worked at the time; everything revolved around their willingness to cooperate. And if you didn't cooperate in their sports system, you could lose your chance to ever study at a university, you could lose your chance at ever being employed and having a job. And not only you, but your siblings, your brothers and sisters, your parents. Basically, all your relatives could become almost stateless people."

With tears in her eyes, Adrea Eife, one of the swimmers Strenk befriended, spoke of the dilemma.

"You are lucky in the West. You can walk away from the sport at any time. It is not so easy for us. If you were us, what would you do?"[34]

While East Germans lived in fear of their government, in the USA, even amiable *Swimming World* magazine carried a classified ad in the early '70s, urging readers to contact their member of Congress to protest escalation of the Vietnam War. Citizens in the West were expanding in thought and expression—whether the leaders of the nation liked it or not—while at every turn, the East was seeking to keep its people under control.

Intersecting the larger political pressures were the lives of ordinary people. Young swimmers, like Kornelia Ender and

Petra Thümer, as well as their parents, team medical doctors, and professional coaches were connected to the East German political milieu through the national sport and the doping program in ways that only now are being understood. Ines Geipel points out that everyone in the dictatorship of Erich Honecker had worth in the sport system. Doctors, coaches, trainers were all connected to the larger goal of elevating the status of East Germany through sport.

It seems three powerful forces influenced the leaders of the East Germany to make the shift from sport and recreation for the good of the citizenry toward the goal of steroid-fueled dominance in Olympic sport.

Foremost, at a very basic level, the "Command Economy" of the Communist regime was failing. Reliable automobiles and adequate housing were scarce to say nothing of staples such as fresh fruits and vegetables and a quality cup of coffee.

One East German swimmer recalls the times in the most realistic conditions.

"When I was on the national team, my family had oranges," she remembers. "When I was not on the national team, they did not have oranges."

In contrast, kids in the USA took much for granted. Day-in and day-out, USA swimmers lived in American economic abundance. Far from any kind of scarcity of oranges, the grocery stores in Southern California where Shirley Babashoff and the Animals trained, like every grocery in America, were stocked with fresh, affordable citrus year-round.

Shortly after the Wall was constructed, West German chancellor Willy Brandt predicted that, in the end, it would be the economy of the West that would eventually compel the Eastern Bloc to open its borders and rejoin the rest of the world. [35]

The second factor was that Germany, a country of proud people, found itself a pariah among nations after World War II. Adolph Hitler's vision of German world dominance had led to the death of millions of Russians—which led to the third significant influence: Communist Russia oversaw East Germany. As Ines Geipel points out, East Germany sought some measure of its own glory, but not just against the West.

A failing economy, the need for nationalistic pride among the citizenry, and pushback against the notion that East Germany was nothing but a puppet state of the Soviet Union all contributed to the doping program.

People will argue the virtue of political and economic systems, whether one system is superior in serving people and aiding them in the pursuit of secure, productive lives, but the fact of the matter is that, from its very formation, the citizens of East Germany wanted to get out.

The Berlin Wall became a symbol for the totalitarian nature of the Communist regime. Over the years East Berliners hid in the trunks of cars, dug secret tunnels and crawled through sewers to make their way to freedom in West Berlin. During a visit to Berlin, President John F. Kennedy famously observed that while capitalism was not a perfect system, democratic nations had never been forced to build a wall to keep their people from leaving.

In some of the most notorious ways, the sport of swimming was destined to be intertwined with East Germany—and not just at the Olympic Games. As it turns out, a swimmer was involved in one of the boldest escapes to freedom.

On the night of August 17, 1969, nineteen-year-old Axel Mitbauer, a 400 freestyle specialist and member of the East German national swim team, slipped into the frigid waters of the Baltic Sea to attempt his getaway. Mitbauer had no Berlin Wall to contend with, but the resort harbor of Boltenhagen was considered part of the frontier border, and as such East German security forces guarded it at all times. Mitbauer timed his crossing of two near-shore sandbars to coincide with the hourly shutdown of the harbor searchlights, which needed periodic cooling.

In sixty-four degree water, Mitbauer swam north and east toward the international shipping lanes and the coast of Western Germany. Twenty-five kilometers and eight hours later, in the early hours of the morning, Mitbauer pulled himself onto a navigational buoy to rest and warm himself in the morning sun. A West German ship discovered him around 7 a.m. and brought him safely to the port of Travemüende.

As if East Germany needed a darker characterization for the doping program, Dr. Werner Franke points out the "Orwellian trick" as he calls it, referring to George Orwell's dystopian world in the novel *1984*. "You use a different word," Dr. Franke points out. "You create a word [to hide the truth]."

Coaches and doctors who were defendants in the doping trials twenty-five years after the Montreal Games replied to questioning, "No, we did not use doping agents. We had just 'supporting means.'"

"It's remarkable," Franke concludes, "how the word becomes important in such secret undertakings."

From the disingenuous characterization of anabolic steroid doping as "supporting means" down to the outright lies that trusted coaches told underage athletes, State Planning Theme 14.25 was diseased.

"Of all the known side effects of doping," says Franke the renowned research biologist with matter-of-fact sarcasm, "lying is the most universally observed." [36]

In the years leading up to the Montreal Olympics, the effects of the doping program in international swimming were clear. In 1968, East German women held only 4.7 percent of the top 25 rankings in swimming events. By the 1972 Games in Munich the number had more than doubled to 10.7 percent. At the end of the summer of 1975, just twelve months prior to the Montreal Games, the number had doubled again, standing at 22.85 percent. Even more telling is the number of top-five rankings in the world during this time frame: In 1968, of the fourteen events contested in swimming, a total of two East German athletes were ranked in the top five; in 1972 just six. By the end of 1976, the number was thirty-five. East Germans women ended 1976 ranked first in every individual event except the 200 breaststroke.

Between the initial doping of the woman shot putter in Mexico City and the 1976 Olympics in Montreal, East German doctors, scientists, and coaches worked to perfect the doping protocols. As one coach from the USA put it, "It looks like they decided if a little anabolic steroid was good for performance, then a lot of anabolic steroid would be even better."

Chapter 8

THE WORLD COMES TO CALI

UPON ARRIVING IN THE SOUTH AMERICAN CITY of Cali, Colombia, for the second swimming World Championships in 1975, Kornelia Ender and her teammates held the world record in nine swimming events. East Germany's cloak of secrecy was tight around the athletes, and the level of control was astounding.

"Under no circumstances," said one of the architects of the doping program to his superiors, "are the women swimmers to give recorded interviews on television."

For the fraud to be effectively maintained, it was important for the East German swimmers to be kept under wraps as much as possible. Manly voices and peculiar physical appearance were best kept away from the eyes of a worldwide viewing public.

With Belgrade and Concord still fresh in their memories, the Americans knew full well what to expect from the East Germans. For their part, the USA coaches had also learned the hard lesson of treating the World Championships as a second-class event. After the Belgrade debacle, the USA leadership determined to focus their full attention on the World Championships by holding a qualifying meet.

The World Championship Trials elevated the perception of the World Championships with the media and the public, as well as with swimmers and coaches. Most coaches, though, did not like the timing of the meet. Most 50-meter pools were outdoors, so many teams had limited access to training in long-course facilities until the weather warmed in mid-May, and coaches did not like the idea of a full taper in June, especially just one year out from the Olympics. As a result, some of America's top athletes did not participate. Kim Peyton and Jill Sterkel sat out the 1975 World Championships in order to have a full summer of training.

The World Championship Trials were held in Long Beach, California, and were followed by a full four-week training camp in Southern California.

As the summer of 1975 came into view, Kathy Heddy was training well. She'd had a bout of mono in the spring that left

Kathy Heddy flanked by East Germany's Ulrike Tauber and Angela Franke.
(Photo credit: Swimming World Magazine)

her weak for the Spring Nationals in Cincinnati, Ohio. But as June approached she was as strong as she'd ever been.

If her parents had been of a certain inclination, Kathy Heddy might have been the kid you see on Broadway, singing "Tomorrow" in Annie. She was small and blonde, pixie-cute. She had a dazzling smile and what her coach, Frank Elm, referred to as a captivating personality. She'd grown up close enough to New York City that the family might have taken her in a different direction, but thankfully for the USA, she chose swimming.

In the absence of Kim Peyton, Shirley and Kathy led the USA women's squad. Shirley's international experience was second to none on the USA team. So regardless of whom the women's team voted as team captain at any competition, Shirley was the defacto leader.

After the trials, the team trained together in Buena Park, California, made a few trips to the beach and met the USA men's team for an afternoon at Disneyland, prior to traveling to Colombia. Even though the women were separated from the men's team, Kathy remembers the training camp as fun and a great bonding experience.

It seems strange that Jack Nelson, who'd been named as the women's head Olympic coach the previous fall, was not included on the coaching staff for the World Championships. Instead, Flip Darr, Shirley's former coach, was named to lead the women's team as head coach. He was about as different from Mark Schubert as any coach could be. He was a man who laughed a lot, preferred plaid shorts and occasionally smoked a pipe while he coached swim practice.

One of America's brightest young coaches, Jack Ridley, was Darr's assistant coach. Ridley coached a string of the USA's top distance swimmers including Jo Harshbarger, who had held the world record in the 800 free and 1,500 free for a time in 1973 and 1974.

"We trained in specialty groups," Ridley remembers. "There was no real talk of the East Germans, but the girls were businesslike. They knew the task before them better now after two big meets with the East Germans, and they worked hard to prepare." The other strategy the coaches employed was to provide the women swimmers with a sport psychology course that included visualization exercises. After the Cali World Championships, Al Schoenfield would scoff at the notion that this kind of program would help in the uphill battle against East Germany. [37]

Cali sits at about 3,000 feet in elevation in the foothills of the Andes Mountains. It is a city described as lush, and temperate, enjoying "perpetual spring." But no corner of the globe was free from general unrest in the early '70s, and Cali was no different.

At the same time that huge crowds flocked to watch the competition, student demonstrations were also going on in the streets. Water polo matches had to be rescheduled at more secure sites, and armed police stood guard around the swimming venue.

The Colombians were either hot or cold toward the visiting American team. While the student protests raged, throngs of friendly Colombians seeking autographs mobbed the team whenever they loaded or unloaded the team bus.

Coach Darr took to diverting the crowds of Colombian autograph seekers by pointing at thirty-two-year-old assistant coach Ridley (who sported thick, dark hair and a heavy dark mustache) and yelling, "Mark Spitz! Mark Spitz!"[38]

The USA women swimmers knew what to expect from the East Germans this time around. To some extent, as Shirley's meet went, so went the meet for the rest of the USA team. She had two races in Cali that would serve as effective dress rehearsals for Montreal a year later. On Wednesday, in what would be a classic battle of racing styles and strategies, Shirley faced Kornelia in the 200 free. And on the following Saturday, Shirley swam both the prelims of the 800 free and the anchor leg on the USA's 4x100-free relay. She won the 200 free and the 400 free, finished third in the 800 behind Australian Jenny Turall and USA teammate Heather Greenwood, and anchored both of the USA's silver medal-winning relays.

Charismatic Kathy Heddy continued to assert herself as one of the world's top swimmers. By far, Kathy swam the widest range of events of any swimmer at Cali. She won the 200 IM against the East Germans, finished third to two East Germans in the 400 IM and led off the USA in the 4x100-free relay.

In the years since East German coaches and medical doctors began administering steroids to athletes, Kornelia Ender had transformed her own swimming style through countless hours of focused repetition.

Of Kornelia one reporter wrote after the World Championships, "[T]here is a beautiful fluidity and swiftness that creates a symphony in motion."[39]

She opened the meet by leading off East Germany's 4x100-free relay and lowering her own world record for the eighth consecutive time. At this point in women's freestyle sprinting, Kornelia Ender stood alone as the only woman to ever swim under 57 seconds. Her split of 56.22 opened up an insurmountable lead. In round three of their epic battle in the relay, the East Germans took back the world record from the USA, winning by more than a second.

The bright spot on the USA's relay was Shirley's anchor split. She chased the East Germans gaining a full second with her fastest 100 ever at 56.71, second only to Kornelia among all the relay swimmers.

Kornelia won four World Titles in Cali. She won the 100 free, the 100 butterfly, and helped the East Germans win both relays. Over the nine-day meet, her only hiccup in an otherwise dominating performance was her rematch with Shirley in the 200 free.

Kornelia scorched the first 100 meters, leading Shirley and the rest of the field by more than two body lengths. At the 125 Shirley's characteristic negative-split strategy had cut Ender's lead in half. Shirley's peculiar hitch in her breathing stroke, the slight head shake at the top of her breath when she accelerated in a race, came as she pushed off the wall with 50 meters to go.

Watching from the stands, Mark Schubert had seen the little head shake dozens of times as she'd raced the top men and women at home in the Animal Lane over the previous three years. In Cali, he knew Shirley had the race in hand at the 150-meter wall.

"I knew Shirley could do it just before the final turn. Just as Kornelia approached the turn, her turnover began to slow down. . . . Shirley swam exactly what she planned. She wanted to be out in a minute. The only difference was we sort of thought Ender would be out in 58 high, not 58 low. I was sort of glad Shirley didn't have to swim right next to Ender. That way she was able to feel her own race," Schubert said afterward.[40]

The rest of the meet would play out mostly as the '73 World Championships had, with the East Germans emerging once again as the pre-eminent team in the world. But Shirley Babashoff and Kathy Heddy would take some confidence from the meet.

The 200 free would prove to be the dueling ground where Shirley and Kornelia, the two foremost swimmers of the age, would battle it out. Kornelia, close to being a pure sprinter, was just plain too fast for Shirley in the 100. While Shirley plowed through mile after mile of over-distance training, Kornelia had taken to refining her sprint racing skills. Kornelia blew away the competition on the start. Both swimmers' turns were horrendously bad, each coming off the wall shallow and sloppy. But Ender's turns were no worse than Shirley's. For her part, Shirley had amazing range. She was just too dominant for Kornelia at the longer events of 400 meters and 800 meters. After the meet, Shirley Babashoff's record in the 200 free against Kornelia Ender stood at two wins and only one loss since their initial meeting in Belgrade.

This time, the USA had committed to an intensive training camp prior to the meet and sent most of its top squad to

Cali. But the East Germans emerged even more dominant at Cali than they had been in Belgrade because of their depth. They won ten of the fourteen swimming events and placed swimmers in the top three in all but two. Without question, the East German program of identifying and training up to five individuals who could possibly win Olympic medals, coupled with steroid doping, was working.

As the meet comes to a close, Al Schoenfield of Swimming World magazine sits in a lengthy interview with Gert Barthelmes, the general secretary of East German swimming. Schoenfield frames an early question in such a way as not to offend, but he is direct.

"Have any teams accused you of taking drugs, or anything illegal?"

"This time they didn't try to attack us with these things. The last attack was done last year at the European Championships."

Feeling pretty confident after more than a week of dominance in the pool, the general secretary elaborates for the benefit of Schoenfield's American audience. The East Germans have always supported doping testing at major championships, he continues. They believe this is the most fair way to assure clean sport. At this point, the general secretary may have implored Schoenfield with outstretched hands.

"As you know the other day they made that test and nobody on our team tested positive."

In what may have been an early attempt to stave off the institution of out-of-competition drug testing, Barthelmes lobbies for the common sense of testing at major competitions.

"We always try to get this doping control when the race is actually done. This is the way we want to show that none of our sportsmen take any drugs."

By 1975 it appears that East German physicians had come close to perfecting the right time to take the swimmers off of steroids to avoid detection.

It may be that Schoenfield spent so much time interacting with honest, middle-class American swimmers and coaches that he was unprepared to question the lies of the Germans.

Whatever the case may be, whether USA coaches and journalists, operating in the vacuum of only circumstantial evidence and rumors, were simply unable to bring themselves to seriously question what was happening, or if the East German officials and coaches became compelling and adept at concealing the truth, the interview comes to a close.

In his analysis of the Cali World Championships, Schoenfield searches for answers. The East Germans specialize and limit the number of events their top competitors swim at international competitions. Officials would confirm a year out from Montreal that Kornelia Ender would swim only the 100 and 200 freestyle, the 100 fly and both relays at Montreal. Shirley, Kathy Heddy and the other top USA swimmers, Schoenfield points out, will swim whatever events they qualify for.

Finally he scolds the USA coaches for their foray into sports psychology prior to Cali. In the face of the daunting task ahead of the Americans in Montreal versus the East Germans, he concludes, "It will take more than a 'self-image psychology' course as given to the American swimmers in California prior to their departure to Cali to narrow the margin."[41]

Chapter 9

SPRING 1976

WENDY LANSBACH HAD RETIRED from swimming in the summer of 1975. She was busy finishing up her under-graduate degree and planning her wedding to Bernie Boglioli, her Monmouth College teammate. While Wendy was at Monmouth, Bernie had taken up coaching with Bill Palmer at Central Jersey Aquatics after graduating the previous spring. The only thing that could have gotten in the way of the couple's plan for the start of normal married life was Bill Palmer.

Early in the fall of '75 with the Olympic Trials just nine months away, Palmer, Bernie's boss at Central Jersey Aquatic's north team, boldly suggested to Wendy that she could earn a spot on the 1976 Olympic Team. With Bernie's encouragement and support, Wendy was back in the water the next day.

Wendy Lansbach Boglioli swam in her first National Championship in Concord California, 1974. *(Photo credit: Swimming World Magazine)*

Before the NCAA included women's swimming as a cham-pionship sport, the Association for Intercollegiate Athlet-ics for Women (AIAW) was the only recognized collegiate championship. Competing and racing during the year for Monmouth, while training with Bill Palmer was a perfect recipe, and Wendy had made huge progress in her college career. Just a month before the USA Nationals she'd won the AIAW Championship in the 100 butterfly in American record time.

The Spring National Championship of 1976 was the final major swim meet before the Olympic Trials. Most of the top coaches, unwilling to interrupt training for the Trials, held normal practices right up until the start of the meet. The championship was held at the Belmont Plaza pool in Long Beach, the same pool where the Olympic Trials would be held in June.

The USA's top stars were slow because they were competing during heavy training, but they raced well. Kim Peyton, who rested only on the day of travel to the meet, touched out Shirley Babashoff to win the 100 freestyle. Jill Sterkel and Sue Hinderaker, both coached at El Monte by Don LaMont, finished third and fourth. The win over Shirley was a boost for Kim's confidence.

"I was surprised, but I knew it was possible," Kim said. "Shirley usually comes up on me in the last 25 meters. With 20 meters to go, she still came up on me, but I was ready for her."

Mark Schubert, though, wasn't impressed with the women's performances. With an eye always on the East Germans, he said, "We sure lulled the world to sleep with this meet," even after his team won its fourth straight national championship.

Pressed by reporters to speculate on the USA's prospects

against the world record holder, Kornelia Ender, Kim took the opportunity to bolster her teammate, Shirley Babashoff.

"Ender's still quite a way off for me," Kim said. "With a proper taper, though, I think I can do a 56 ... and so can Shirley." [42]

The only real surprise on the women's side was Wendy Lansbach Boglioli. At age twenty-one, she continued her steep trajectory of improvement, winning the 100 butterfly in a new American Record time.

One of seven children born to parents of German descent, Wendy's summer training regimen as a kid included continuous swims around the Wisconsin lake near her home. The Lansbach family from Land O' Lakes, Wisconsin, had to be creative. In the winter Wendy trained in the 17-yard-long pool at the hotel where her father worked as the hotel engineer. Her dad learned his trade during a stint in the US Army during World War II, and he was a tinkerer. Wendy trained in the ultra short hotel pool tethered to a weight stack by a harness her father constructed.

During the long winter, he would also construct a brand new starting block, and as soon as the water became a reasonable swimming temperature, he would set out a 50-meter course in the lake for proper Olympic-distance training.

Using clothesline and hand-crafted square wood floats positioned at 1-meter intervals, the seven Lansbach kids, "the tribe" as they came to refer to themselves, and a handful of hardy kids from nearby towns, would begin their "long course" training in the lake, in preparation for summer swim meets.

At the age of thirteen, Wendy recalls walking the five blocks to the Land O' Lakes Public library to check out Doc Counsilman's *The Science of Swimming*. It turns out she was, like her parents, a student of the sport. She remembers finishing the book cover to cover in short order.

While video from the '70s shows many of the top sprinters with ferocious arm recoveries coupled with high-tempo stroke rates, Wendy's stroke is different, a product it seems of the engineering of her German parents. They read everything they could get their hands on related to competitive swimming. When the kids went to clean out the attic of the A-frame home where they grew up, they found every *Swimming World* magazine from issue number one onward.

Wendy's mother coached her and laid a foundation that stressed perfect technique in her developing years. Wendy recalls that her mother was a woman ahead of her time. "During the war, when Major League Baseball had to shut down, my mom made $400 a month playing catcher on the Wisconsin Cardinals, a St. Louis Cardinals semi-pro women's team."

"I remember sitting in the warmth of our little chalet style house on a dark Wisconsin evening and my mom was talking to us kids. At one point she turned to me, pointing a wooden spoon she'd been stirring stew with. 'Wendy,' she said in her determined German mother way, 'some day soon there will be scholarships for women to play sports in college.'"

With little in the way of resources, the Lansbachs used what they had available to them and invented a competitive swim team out of thin air. At the height of the program the tiny team had only fourteen swimmers. Incredibly, out of this small group emerged Wendy, a USA Olympian, her sister Laurie, also a world-class swimmer, and Karen Reeder (Burton), an NCAA Division 2 National Champion for the Air Force Academy, who eventually swam the English Channel and won a bronze medal at the 1991 world championships in 25 kilometers.

"I did not know what I was getting myself into," Wendy says of her training with Bill Palmer, "but as soon as I met him I loved him." Palmer was a perfect coach for her when she needed a push beyond her comfort zone in order to get to the next level. Like Mark Schubert, Palmer oversaw eight lanes of swimmers with unerring attention to detail. [43]

"We tried to stay up with what was going on in California at Mission Viejo. It was like an arms race, to see who could do the most volume," said Palmer of Wendy's training program. [44]

It may have helped a bit that Palmer ran the family trash hauling business. There is nothing like having a coach with a small chip on his shoulder to fuel a passion for greatness among the athletes. Not only was the Central Jersey team not basking in the sun of the Golden State, their coach showed up for early morning practice after making sure the garbage trucks had completed their rounds. But cracking the perception that only California produced "real" swimmers was a formidable task.

Mark Schubert and the Animals at Mission Viejo get much of the credit for changing the training paradigm of the times, but by the spring of 1976 the swimming world was full of Animal Lanes. From New Jersey to Oregon, almost all teams were training two to three hours in the pool, twice a day. Right up the 405 freeway from Mission Viejo, Dick Jochums helped place just as many swimmers on the 1976 team as Mark Schubert did. Veteran performers like Steve Furniss trained at Jochums' Beach Swim Club alongside his brother Bruce and freestyle high school phenom Tim Shaw, who at one point in 1975 held the world record in every freestyle event from the 200 to the 1,500.

Unlike track and other land sports, swimming occurs in an essentially weightless environment, with the body being constantly cooled. Without the limitations of gravity and heat build-up, coaches in the '70s soon found that their best athletes were capable of enormous workloads.

When swimmers and coaches from the era talk about those days, the magic number is 20,000 meters a day. Even among the East Germans, when Kornelia Ender reaches back in her memory, she speaks of training 20,000 meters during the heaviest training periods. No one says they swam 25,000 or 15,000 per day. It is always 20,000 as though it was a human threshold beyond which no swimmer could survive.

The fact is the Animals rarely swam 20,000 meters in a day. What they did do was between 6,500 and 8,500 meters for eleven practices per week. And whether he thought of it in these terms, Schubert periodized his training through the competitive season. The months of June and January, roughly eight weeks out from the Spring and Summer Nationals, came in at the high end, around 90,000 meters per week.

Virtually every program that was producing top swimmers in the USA in the '70s was doing it in part through high volume. As early as the 1972 American Swim Coaches Convention, a spirited debate was brewing between coaches who favored high volume and those who thought higher quality, with less emphasis on total volume was the way to go. What gets lost in the age-old swimming debate of volume versus quality is the sheer speed of the volume that swimmers were accomplishing daily in the Animal Lane. Shirley Babashoff's set of three 800s that concluded with a swim just 2 seconds over the world record was at the far end of the spectrum, but even so, Babashoff, Brian Goodell, and the rest of the Animals regularly swam times in a series of mile repeats that would score in the top eight at the National Championships.

By the spring of 1976 Mission Viejo had attracted swimmers from all over the world who believed that training with the Animals was the best way to prepare for Montreal. In March, Dutch swimmers Enith Brigitha and Annelies Maas came to train at Mission Viejo. Enith, at five-foot-eleven, was probably the most physically gifted of the world's top sprinters. At Belgrade she had finished third in the 100 freestyle behind Kornelia and Shirley and at Cali she tied Shirley for second place. Enith had an enormous wingspan and great feel for the water in the front-end of her stroke.

Standing waist-deep in the Caribbean Ocean along the coast of her home on the island of Curaçao in what was then known as the Netherland Antilles, Enith's mother taught her to swim. After immigrating to Holland, Enith began swimming with Willie Storm, who became like a second mother to her and helped her become one of the best freestyle sprinters in the world. Later, Enith's desire to compete against the best in workout settings led to the decision to train at Mission Viejo in the spring of '76.

Enith remembers the high volume and camaraderie of the team: "It was fun to have a large group training together toward one goal. Mark Schubert would always get us together before the practice and tell us what the emphasis for the practice was that day. Of course when I returned to Holland in May, I had to regain some of the speed that was missing after all the training."[45]

If Ines Geipel is correct when she observes that behind every great sports story is a motivating story, then the story-behind-the-story for many of the swimmers in the Animal Lane is one of near obsession driven perhaps by a feeling of being an outsider. Mission Viejo was a community of doctors, lawyers, real estate developers, and individuals in the financial industry.

Brian Goodell's father, Wayne, by contrast, worked long, physical days as a contractor. Top American breaststroker Marcia Morey and backstroker Maryanne Graham came from out of state and boarded with Mission Viejo families so they could train with the Animals. Enith and Annelies, along with two of Great Britain's best swimmers, Jim Carter and Brian Lonsdale, who came to Mission Viejo to tune up for Montreal, surely felt like outsiders training 5,000 miles from home. And as New York Times sportswriter Karen Crouse observed, Shirley had a bit of a chip on her shoulder.

Babashoff commuted 30 miles from working-class Fountain Valley to Mission Viejo every day. Her family was not upper-class, observes Crouse. Her father worked hours of overtime to keep the kids in swimming.

"I think that was part of what gave Shirley her edge," Crouse says. "She felt like she was from the 'wrong side of the tracks' in swimming."[46]

Without question, the Animal Lane was populated with individuals who had something to prove, and it seems no task that Mark Schubert could lay before them was too great. The work bound them together, and a synergy emerged among the group that Schubert never quite achieved again in his coaching career.

In his first years of coaching in Akron, Schubert dealt with the most difficult event a young coach can face when one of his young swimmers, Charlie Stewart, was accidently electrocuted during a swim practice. Long before coaches were trained in CPR and sports facilities were equipped with automatic heart defibrillators, 12-year-old Charlie Stewart died in Schubert's arms after stepping on a grate that had been electrified when workmen allowed an extension cord to be pinched in the hinges.[47]

The Animals, almost all of whom felt like outsiders in some way, were bound together with a man with a traumatic event in his past. It seems all of them had something to prove, and the sport of swimming was the avenue they chose to travel together. In the spring of 1976 the challenges for Shirley Babashoff reached a peak that threatened to overwhelm her.

While Mark Schubert insists that he had nothing but a positive relationship with Shirley's mother, it must have come as a surprise to Vera Babashoff when Shirley came home from practice just weeks after the Spring Nationals and announced that she was quitting.

"I quit swimming right before the Olympic Trials. For maybe like a day, and I went to the beach.

"And then I came home from the beach and Mark Schubert's car is in our driveway. And I'm like, *Uh-oh. I'm in trouble.*"[48]

Schubert's intuition had been correct: The constant attention from the press, the constant questions about the East Germans and the comparisons to Kornelia Ender were taking their toll on Shirley. As the Olympic Trials got closer, she was in the paper almost every day.

"At that time I had been in the paper so much when I was 19, I felt like I was 19 for 20 years because every time you look in the paper it said your name and your age. So you're constantly looking that you're 19, you're 19, you're 19. I just wanted to be normal so badly," Shirley recalled.

Sitting on the couch in the Babashoffs' living room, all Mark Schubert really pointed out to Shirley was that it was not good for her to quit after all the work she had put into preparing for Montreal.

"I don't want you to be known as the girl who quit right before the Olympics."[49]

Shirley was back at practice the next day.

With the Olympic Trials just weeks away and the Montreal Games beyond that, the task before Shirley Babashoff, Kim Peyton, Wendy Boglioli, and the other USA women was daunting. They had no control over the East Germans; all they could do was put the finishing touches on their final weeks of preparation.

Chapter 10

SHIRLEY'S MEET

IT WAS AMERICA'S BICENTENNIAL, and maybe only Elton John could have pulled off the number one hit "Philadelphia Freedom," the kind of song that can get stuck in a swimmer's head during a long swim set to the point of temporary insanity. With the Elton John production, trilling flutes and all playing in the background, Schubert took the microphone at an exhibition practice leading up to the Trials in Long Beach. He spoke about each swimmer who would compete in the upcoming trials. The Mission Viejo Company, which sponsored Schubert's top group, had invited the community to see the swim team up close and in action. It was like an afternoon engagement at SeaWorld, the aquatic creatures endlessly and effortlessly streaking down the pool, flipping and

Shirley and coach Mark Schubert at the '76 Olympic Trials at the Belmont Plaza pool.
(Photo credit: Swimming World Magazine)

streaking back. All the coach lacked was a sardine treat at the end of each lane.

As many as a dozen of the Mission Viejo swimmers had a legitimate shot at the Olympic team. Mark Schubert's Mission Viejo team was a mixture of Southern California kids and the imports from all over the USA and abroad. They were near famous in the lead-up to the Trials in the community, so that many of the swimmers at the exhibition were familiar names. Shirley, of course, was already a household name. On the men's side, sixteen-year-old Brian Goodell was on the cusp of a historic run at the Trials and two gold medals at the Olympics. Brian was unique because he was the only one of the Animals who'd come up through the Mission Viejo club ranks as an age grouper. In all, six swimmers from the team would qualify for the Montreal Olympics. Of the locals, Brian and Shirley, the superstars, were joined on the USA team by Marcia Morey, Maryanne Graham, and fourteen-year-old Nicole Kramer.

The freight train of the super-era of women's swimming that had started to roll at the Dallas Nationals in '74 came steaming into the Belmont Plaza Pool in Long Beach at full speed, never slowing but continually gaining momentum through the six-day meet. The USA Olympic Trials have traditionally been the most competitive swim meet in the world in every Olympic year. The sheer depth of talent in the USA in all events eclipses any other nation two to one. And there are always surprises at the meet.

Of the big surprises at the Olympic Trials in Long Beach— the first of the goggles era—Karen Moe Thornton won the

200 butterfly. Over the week of spring break in her senior year at UCLA, Karen had married Mike Thornton. Even though she had retired, for the second time after the women's AIAW meet earlier in the spring, out of habit perhaps, she noted that the winning time in the 200 butterfly at the Spring Nationals was slower than the time she had swum to win the gold medal in Munich four years earlier. With very little time remaining before the closing of entries for the Trials, she went into training with her old coach, George Haines, who was now coaching the men at UCLA, and qualified to swim at the Olympic Trials.

Unfortunately, the USA took a step backward when Kathy Heddy arrived at the meet suffering from a back injury most typically seen in baseball pitchers. Her coach, Frank Elm, noticed the change in her strokes immediately. Kathy, who might have been in contention for as many as five medals in Montreal, struggled to make the team in the 400 freestyle only.

Young Jill Sterkel made the team on the first day of the meet by swimming to a surprising third place finish in the 200 freestyle. Jill, like Kim Peyton, was beloved by her teammates and the people in her local community. When she arrived home after making the team, family friends in her Hacienda Heights neighborhood had covered the front porch with rose petals.

Wendy Boglioli had added strength and endurance to her textbook technique through a nine-month regimen of weight training and crushing swim practices with Bill Palmer. But three weeks prior to the Trials, she suffered a bursitis attack in her shoulder that required her to rest from full stroke swimming. For almost three weeks she only kicked through most practices. Ironically, both her husband, Bernie, and coach Palmer considered this as one of the key elements to her success at the Trials. The injury provided the necessary rest she needed to recover and be ready to race at full capacity. Wendy's father attributed it to divine intervention: "It's God's way of telling you that you need rest." Whatever the source of the bursitis, Wendy finished second behind Camille Wright's American Record swim in the 100 butterfly to earn a spot on the '76 team.

It is hard to grasp Shirley's dominance of the '76 Olympic Trials. The meet started on a Wednesday and went right through the weekend to the following Monday. She started the meet by winning the 200 free in American Record time. On day two, in what must have been a surprise even to the ultra confident Babashoff, she won the 400 Individual Medley, an event not considered one of her best. On day three she dominated the field by over 4 seconds to win the 400 free in an American Record.

On Sunday, the top four finishers in the 100 freestyle decided the 4x100-free relay. Going into the race, Olympic head coach Jack Nelson could hope for a USA dream team in the 4x100-freestyle relay in Montreal. He could dream of three recent American Record holders in Kim Peyton, Kathy Heddy, and Shirley Babashoff. The fourth spot would be a wild card of sorts. Perhaps Jill Sterkel, whose split at the Pan American Games in the summer of 1975 had saved the victory in the free relay. Clearly, she thrived in high-pressure situations, particularly when the team needed her. But any number of other swimmers might step up at the Trials and claim one of the top four finishes in the 100 free to assure a spot on the relay team. Nelson's own swimmer, Bonnie Brown from Fort Lauderdale, might be the next most likely, but all across the country swimmers had been pushing their own limits, adapting to higher workloads and perfecting skills in dreams of making the team.

After three years of the American Record swapping back and forth between Kim, Kathy, and Shirley, at the Trials Shirley established herself as the anchor for both the 4x100-medley relay and the 4x100-free relays in Montreal by winning the 100 freestyle in American Record time. Jill Sterkel, Kim Peyton, and Wendy Boglioli finished 2-3-4.

Kim Peyton had struggled through the Olympic Trials, coming off a bout of flu. When she made the team in the 100 freestyle, it was with a measure of relief. "This was my last chance," she said in *Swimming World*. "I'm very relieved right now. Everything was riding on tonight."

Certainly, elation spread among the twenty-four women who made the USA roster, but the prevailing sentiment of the women on the 1976 women's Olympic team, with the exception of Shirley perhaps, was similar to Kim's—one of relief and gratitude for having made the team in the pressure cooker setting of the Trials.

Years later, Kim's husband, Drew McDonald, would use the word "electric" to describe Kim. One of her gifts, McDonald would remember, was her ability to bring people together. After the final of the 100 free in Long Beach, with no regard for her own prospects for an individual medal in Montreal, she spun the enormous task before herself and her teammates in the most positive light. [50]

"I'm sure we can all come down and beat the East German relay team," she said. [51]

Jack Nelson now had his freestyle relay team. Fifteen-year-old Jill Sterkel, whose first big international meet was the '75 Pan Am Games the summer before, and twenty-one-year-old Wendy Boglioli, whose first international competition would be the Montreal Olympics, would join the veterans Peyton and Babashoff on the relay. Kim and Shirley had both been tested and toughened over the four years of international competition between Munich and Montreal. Sterkel and Boglioli would have only one month of pre-Olympic training camp to prepare for the pressures of the Games.

Even though Kornelia Ender was in a class by herself as the world's fastest woman by almost a full second, the USA would be just as strong, or perhaps stronger, in sprint freestyle than the next three East German sprinters. If they held a strategy meeting, Nelson and his assistant coaches might have seen the freestyle relay at the Montreal Olympics as an opportunity for an upset.

By Sunday evening, everyone at Belmont Plaza understood that the conductor of the record-breaking train was Shirley Babashoff. She always raced in black goggles, whether indoors or out. Before the 800 freestyle she swung her goggles carelessly back and forth on her index finger. So confident and relaxed was she on the last day of the Olympic Trials that moments before the final of the 800, she sat behind the blocks in a folding chair stretching an arm overhead, letting out a great gaping yawn.

Her transformation into the world's best distance swimmer is one of the most remarkable journeys in the history of swimming. In Munich, she swam the 100 and 200 freestyles. Over the course of the next four years, Shirley moved up in distance to become the world record holder in both the 400 and 800 meters. While it is common for track and field athletes to move up in distance as their sprint speed diminishes, for a world-class swimmer it is unheard of.

Apart from Mark Spitz, no swimmer in history, not even Kornelia Ender, had dominated a major swimming competition as completely as Shirley did at Long Beach. She swam American Records in the 100, 200, 400 freestyles, set the world record in the 800 free and tacked on a first place finish in the 400 IM. In the absence of steroid-enhanced performances by the doped East Germans, presumably, all of Shirley's freestyle times would have been world records.

As the team assembled at the far end of the Belmont Plaza Pool for recognition by the California crowd, Shirley Babashoff stood as the central figure on the team, male or female.

The USA team went directly from the Long Beach pool to the airport Marriott after the final event of the Trials. Head Olympic coach Jack Nelson, head assistant Frank Elm, and young Jim Montrella now faced the toughest task any group of USA coaches had ever faced: preparing the USA women's team for an Olympic Games where the deck was stacked against them in ways that would only be fully understood decades later.

1976 United States Olympic Women's Swimming Team (Left to Right): *Back Row* | Frank Elm, Shirley Babashoff, Jill Sterkel, Janis Hape, Jack Nelson, Nicole Kramer, Kathy Heddy Camille Wright, Jim Montrella *Middle Row* | Linda Jezek, Jeanne Haney, Wendy Weinberg, Donnalee Wennerstrom, Jennifer Hooker, Melissa Belote, Maryanne Graham, Laurie Siering, Kim Peyton, Tauna Vandeweghe *Front Row* | Brenda Borgh, Lelei Fonoimoana, Wendy Boglioli, Carol Finneran, Karen Moe Thornton, Marcia Morey, Charlotte Piper, Mirium Smith, Renee Laravie, Renee Magee *(Photo credit: Wendy Boglioli)*

Chapter 11

THE LONG GRAY MONTH

THE OBVIOUS CHOICE FOR HEAD WOMEN'S COACH
for the 1976 team would have been Karen Moe Thornton's
former coach, George Haines. Over the previous decade
at Santa Clara Swim Club, he was the most accomplished
women's coach in America. But he was selected as assistant
coach on the men's squad when the coaches were chosen
at the AAU convention in the fall of 1974. Shirley's coach,
Mark Schubert, was another possible choice, but as a relative
newcomer to the international scene, he was not considered.
So the job of women's head Olympic coach went to jovial, en-
ergetic Jack Nelson from the Fort Lauderdale Swim Team. An
Olympian and silver medalist himself in 1964, Nelson held
the world record in the 400 freestyle at one point for a matter
of hours before rival Don Schollander took it back.

A pioneer swim coach, Nelson was fun loving and an early
proponent of the power of sports psychology and performance self-talk. Supporters in South Florida described Nelson
as a national treasure [52] because he helped bring big-time
swimming and the International Swimming Hall of Fame to
Fort Lauderdale. In a career spanning more than thirty years,
he coached thirty-six Olympians including four gold medalists.

But in the summer of 1976, Nelson's international coaching experience was limited. Prior to taking on the Olympic team, he'd coached the USA women the week of the '74 USA vs. East Germany dual meet, and he had taken a team on a tour of Japan in '75. He had no experience with an elite group of women swimmers in a month-long training camp environment. Jack Nelson's main coaching had been confined to his work with his own top-level club athletes, and none of his swimmers made the team in '76. Bonnie Brown, Nelson's top swimmer, just missed qualifying as a member of the 4x100 relay, finishing fifth in the 100 free behind Shirley, Jill, Kim, and Wendy.

With the Olympic Trials behind them and four weeks of fine-tuning ahead, the women might have gained a little momentum. But then came news from the East German Olympic Trials where Berlin's Dynamo SC , the club where many of the East German Olympians trained, had set the world record in the 4x100-free relay—*without Kornelia Ender.* A world record in the freestyle relay without the reigning world record holder was hard to grasp, but it was just the beginning. At their Olympic Trials, East Germans swam under existing world marks twenty-five times.

The results proved too much for even the eternally optimistic Jack Nelson to overcome with the most positive thinking. Going into the Montreal Games, East Germans held the world record in every Olympic swimming event except Shirley Babashoff's record in the 800 freestyle. To be fair, Jack Nelson faced a dilemma never seen before or since in American swimming: How does a head coach lead the world's most historically dominant team when the margins in many of the races ahead are so great that basic arithmetic begins to tell the tale?

In the first final of the Games, the USA would enter the medley relay in Montreal as 7-second underdogs to the East Germans. As was the case in Belgrade in 1973, the East German relay featured the current world record holder in each of the four strokes, while the USA team was populated by American record holders in three of the four legs, the exception being Shirley, who swam free and was considered the best closer, perhaps in the world. Nelson's USA women faced similar margins of dominance in almost every event they would swim at the Olympics.

Swimming is not a ball sport where coaches and players devise key strategies to neutralize the opposing team's strengths while amplifying their own. In swimming, the racers line up and start together, no clever offense or secretive defense makes a bit of difference. Only subtle race strategies have any effect on the straight-up, one-on-one competition. Epic swim races are more akin to fifteen-round boxing matches—tests of will and confidence and stamina. However, at some point, when the margins are large enough, tenacity has little to do with the outcome.

In 1972 for example, Karen Moe Thornton won the gold medal and set the Olympic record at 2:15.57 in the 200 butterfly. Four years later, after a remarkable comeback, she posted 2:14.23 at the '76 Olympic Trials. Going into Montreal, however, she faced a 3-second deficit as the defending Olympic champion. The USA's top 100 backstroker, Linda Jezek, went into the meet more than three seconds behind on paper.

Even before the Olympic Trials, anyone paying attention could see that not only were the top USA swimmers over-matched, but in many events the East Germans had two or three athletes seeded ahead of them. *Swimming World* magazine put it this way: "Statistically speaking, the American women in the 100 backstroke have to be pretty happy that the [East German] women are limited to just three competitors in this event. Going into the Olympics, the East Germans have seven of the eight top [world] rankings. ..."[53]

It was not just the incredible drops in time that the top East German swimmers had posted over the previous three years that took the world by surprise; it was also the fact that these results were coming from a country roughly the size of the state of Virginia.

Compounding the difficulties that the USA women faced was the fact that Jack Nelson missed something big when it came to the dynamics of the USA women's team. Surprisingly, this motivator of young people somehow failed to connect with a large number of the swimmers. The mood of the team upon their arrival at West Point, New York, for their pre-Olympic training camp was sullen.

While the men's team became the toast of the town in mid-America Canton Ohio, the women's experience was a mixed bag of boredom, disjointed training, and passive-aggressive behaviors that leaned toward rebellion. There were few team meetings. Team chaperone Carol Finneran, who might have been able to add insight into team dynamics, drifted into a school-marmish adversarial role. The older swimmers who had been on previous international teams banded together, leaving the younger ones, whose first big international meet was going to be the Olympic Games, to try to discern from the coaches how to prepare for competition on the biggest stage swimming has to offer.

On top of all that, the messages coming down from the coaches were confusing. Jack coupled his mind-power message with a paternal approach rooted in his rural north Georgia upbringing. "How are you doing this morning ladies?" he would greet the women on the bus. "Everyone sure looks pretty today." It came across as demeaning and inappropriate, especially to the older athletes.

Karen Moe Thornton and others met Nelson's message with skepticism bordering on hostility. The women knew that Jack Nelson's mind-power message was not going to be enough to overcome the time deficits they faced. Nelson, as Karen remembers it, came across as out of touch and unapproachable.[54]

Frank Elm, Jack's second in command, lived within driving distance of the pool at West Point. After practice, he was often quickly out the door so he could make it home for a night's sleep in his own bed rather than stay on campus. He failed to build relationships with the athletes beyond their work-a-day interactions in practices. Jim Montrella, the youngest of the coaches, could see what was happening, but having the least international experience, he felt cut off by Nelson and Elm from any meaningful discussion about the team's preparation.[55]

One of the problems was Shirley. Despite her performances at the Trials, she was high-strung emotionally, facing enormous expectations at the Games, and training for the biggest meet of her life without her coach, Mark Schubert. During the final week of training camp, she would appear on the cover of the Sports Illustrated Games preview issue— along with Frank Shorter, the marathon runner, and basketball star Scott May—billed as America's Gold Medal Hopefuls. Schubert had strongly encouraged her not to accept the cover photo opportunity, but it in the end it was impossible to pass up. Photographed in official team-issued red sweats with the Olympic rings, she was blonde, athletic, and beautiful—the golden girl from Southern California.

But America's girl was facing difficulties that miles and miles of swim training did not prepare her for. Shirley was not a girls-girl, having grown up with brothers and swimming mostly with guys in the Animal Lane, she preferred training with men. She fell into an awkward spot as the most prominent star of the USA swim team. As such, the younger girls revered her and placed her on a pedestal. On the other end, she faced a certain amount of natural jealousy from some of the older team members, each of whom were great athletes in their own right but were dealing with certain obscurity if Shirley had the performance she seemed capable of at the Games.

All of these factors were influenced and intensified by the rumor of anabolic steroids fueling the East German team. It seemed the USA women could find no support anywhere. Even team chaperone Finneran had seen fit to lecture the women's team on good sportsmanship in a *Swimming World* editorial. [56]

Of course much of Shirley's isolation was of her own making. She was brash in her confidence and vocal when something did not seem right to her. The task facing her at the Olympics was unheard of. She would race the entire range of the swimming program at Montreal: the 100, 200, 400, and 800 free. To top it off, as the fastest 100 freestyler at the Trials, she would be called upon to anchor the medley and free relays, and she was the USA's number one qualifier in the 400 individual medley.

No swimmer, male or female, in the history of the sport had ever faced a wider range of physical demands in a single Olympics. At the West Point training camp it appeared the coaching leadership missed all the clues about Shirley and the rest of the team. If the most accomplished woman swimmer in American history was to effectively lead the USA women's team, she needed a connection with the coach.

With Elm disengaged and Nelson a slightly out-of-touch father figure, Shirley became isolated, and dissatisfaction quickly entered the pool. Shirley was unhappy. The girls did not like the practices. They were isolated from family, friends, and their own coaches, and facing looming odds. At West Point, things got petty very quickly. Repeat 800s were stupid, Shirley thought, and she had no problem with expressing it to anyone who would listen. She needed to be sprinting. [57]

Decades later, Frank Elm recalls few details from the training camp, but he is clear about one thing. When Elm says emphatically, "Babashoff was a pain in the ass to coach," there is a certain amount of reverence in his tone, like a sea captain remembering a great storm he'd brought his ship through. [58] Nelson and Elm were well-established coaches at the time and were not accustomed to swimmers questioning their coaching decisions.

Then came rumors of Mark Schubert's involvement. No one can completely agree as to Schubert's role in how the women trained. Some of the swimmers believed Schubert loomed large in the daily practice regimen, directing Elm's group by phone from California. Others believe he stayed in the background, trying his best to stabilize the situation with phone calls to Shirley and the coaches. But the reaction was less than positive. None of the other swimmers' coaches were being consulted; many of the women assumed, then, that the coaches were only concerned about Shirley.

In what may have been the most crippling psychological blow to the seasoned veterans on the team, the women believed that because of the overwhelming odds facing them, some of the top coaches had declined the chance to lead the women's team. [59]

The women of the 1976 Olympic swim team could not catch a break, which even included their living arrangements at training camp. As it happened, the team was stuck on the campus of West Point the very first summer that women were accepted as members of the previously all-male student body. The inclusion of women was one more unsettling event in the turbulent current of American society at the time. So upsetting was this fact to certain West Point grads, that some were said to have mailed back their graduation rings in protest of opening the Point to women. The very atmosphere at West Point seemed unwelcoming and tense.

"All I remember about West Point was rules," recalles Jill Sterkel. Everything was gray. The buildings on the campus were gray. The sky was often gray. Even on a clear morning, gray fog hung in the river bottom below the campus.

The girls made a trip to New York City, but beyond that, the only team-building activity anyone can recall may hold the most telling image of the girls' experience. Asked by team chaperone Finneran to spend the afternoon making door decorations for each of their rooms at the hotel, Karen Moe Thornton and Wendy Boglioli returned from the hardware store with a roll of duct tape. While stars and stripes and photos adorned most of the doors in the hallway, the two senior women stretched a single thick line of gray tape from the top doorjamb to the floor. That long gray line spoke the most accurately of the girls' frustrations during the long gray month of semi-captivity at the Thayer Hotel on the grounds of the U.S. Military Academy. [60]

As if training camp morale was not low enough, at some point the staff decided to institute daily weigh-ins. Swimmers began to lose weight. The women ate all meals at the hotel or at the West Point dining hall. They were not allowed to wear jeans or shorts on the campus or in the mess hall, so they tromped around in the heavy gray cotton sweat suits that were issued to them back in Long Beach. To battle the stifling heat and humidity in the Hudson River Valley, the girls made "shorts" by hiking up the pant legs of their sweats.

Attitudes toward training deteriorated; no one seemed to be swimming very well in practices. While the men were guided by medalists with two and three Olympics under their belt, the most seasoned swimmers on the women's team had started to withdraw.

The one bright spot for the team came just before they left for Montreal. At an exhibition meet held in a short-course 25-yard pool, Jill Sterkel set three American Records leading off the 200-free relay, the 400-free relay and the 800-free relay. Her 100 free at West Point marked the first time a woman had ever swum under 50 seconds. It may have been hard for the coaches to appreciate Jill's surprising achievements in light of the dreary team setting, but they could not have missed her innate competitiveness. Years later she remembers her brash attitude toward the East Germans was simply, "Bring it on!" [61]

When the women's team arrived at the team staging site for the USA athletes at the State University of New York, Platts-burgh, they cheered up a bit. They reunited with the men's team, whose brimming confidence was infectious. The few short days it took to outfit the team and tailor their uniforms was a breath of fresh air for the women swimmers, but it was short-lived. Trouble was threatening the Montreal Games at both the local and geo-political level.

Every host city for an Olympic Games bears the cost of the Games as a civic entity. The infrastructure and security are the responsibility of the local taxpayers, not to mention the construction of an array of state-of-the-art facilities. The Montreal Games were almost the Games that never were. When the city was awarded the Olympics in 1970, it was con-sidered a great coup. At that time, Mayor Jean Drapeau esti-mated the cost at a modest $310 million. After labor strikes, inclement weather, and poor planning, the cost soared to nearly $1.5 billion. As late as the spring of '76 there was talk of moving the Games, or at least moving some of the sports to another location.

Finishing the Olympic venues for the opening ceremonies became a mad scramble. In fact, large portions of the athlete village and Olympic Stadium in Montreal were never completed. The mast on the stadium from which a giant umbrella-like structure was to be lowered to protect the track on a rainy day is still a stubby truncated tower. Canadian Olympic official Dick Pound remembers the sentiment of the times with some amount of hyperbole: "Now it's true that the last workman was backing out of the stadium with a paintbrush as the athlete carrying the Greek flag came in. I mean it was pretty close."[62]

Even though the '75 Pan American Games in Mexico City had been a great success for her, Kim Peyton worried over the prospect of moving the swimming to Mexico if the Montreal swim stadium was not complete. At the Pan Ams, Mexican Nationals had repeatedly booed athletes from the USA simply because they represented America.

The two previous Olympic Games in Mexico and Munich had been marked by the intrusion of politics and violence. Montreal's response was to deploy 16,000 police and military troops, resulting in an athlete village that resembled an armed compound. It was rumored, "ominously" in these days of the Cold War, that there was even a plan in place in case of a nuclear attack.

The '76 Games successfully avoided any violence, but they were marred by the exclusion of nations from Africa to Asia as governments postured for recognition of their grievances, using athletes as visible, expendable pawns.

Many of the best runners in the world were denied the opportunity to compete in Montreal when much of the African continent pulled out of the Games. The African nations were protesting the inclusion of New Zealand at the '76 Games, after that country had allowed its rugby team to compete in apartheid segregated South Africa. Kenya, Egypt, Cameroon, and others packed up their athletes and headed home in reluctant compliance to orders from their governments. Support for the protest spread to the West when tiny Guyana and its delegation, including track star James Gilkes (a student at USC and one of the favorites in the 200), pulled out. Before leaving Canada, Gilkes would petition the International Olympic Committee in an unsuccessful effort to run as a free agent, to "represent Gilkes."[63]

In one of the cruelest shows of political manipulation, the Canadian government turned away athletes from Taiwan at the airport, relenting to pressure from Nationalist China, which took issue with the Taiwanese delegation marching in the opening ceremonies under the flag of The Republic of China. Officials in Peking demanded that only one China could be represented at the Olympics, and it would not be Taiwan. After pledging that any nation recognized by the International Olympic Committee would be allowed to compete in Montreal, Canada changed its policy at the last moment.

Governments from around the globe overrode the notion of friendly competition. This trend would continue through the next two Olympic Games, with President Jimmy Carter's boycott of the 1980 Moscow Games and the '84 boycott by East-Bloc Communist nations in retaliation. Starting in Mexico and Munich, the intrusion of politics would result in world-class athletes being denied a chance at full Olympic competition for the next twelve years. Sadly, the next "full" Olympic Games that would include the entire international Olympic community would be in Seoul, Korea, in 1988.

In the summer of '76, workers were still in the process of cleaning and tidying the swimming facilities when athletes began to arrive. But the pool itself was ready, and it was like no other in the world. The pool would be proclaimed "fast" by '72 swimming superstar Mark Spitz while leading a media tour, and indeed it was.

For the USA women swimmers the chance to get out of the gray training-camp environment of West Point and finally get to Montreal was tempered by the living arrangements. Six thousand athletes from ninety-two nations were housed in four pyramid-shaped apartment buildings constructed across the street from the swim stadium. The problem was there were not enough bedrooms to go around. The USA women's team stayed twelve to each apartment in makeshift arrangements. Six-foot Wendy Boglioli and five-foot-ten Jill Sterkel slept with feet hanging off the end of tiny single beds in what was the dining room of the apartment the girls shared with half their team. The staff made the decision that Shirley and the others who had multiple swims during the week would sleep in the bedrooms with just one or two roommates.

Despite the fact that this team was destined to face challenges no other team would face, they were proud to represent their country. For every member of the team, their lifelong dream was to compete for the USA at the Olympic Games.

Team captain Marcia Morey summed up the feeling of the team in *Swimming World* magazine: "I'm extremely proud to make the Olympic team, just to make the team. ... [I]t's the proudest thing ever in my life." [64]

Chapter 12

MONTREAL: THE 21ST OLYMPIAD

SWIMMING IS A SPORT FUELED by the individual pursuit of speed. It is about the courage to push beyond previous limits with enough regularity to change the body at the cellular level. Mitochondria appear larger and in greater numbers in the cells of highly trained athletes. Capillary branches are developed more densely in the muscle tissue. The capacity of heart, lung, and muscle to process oxygen, and fuel at astounding speed is fine-tuned. The uptake and delivery of oxygen operates at a screaming rate in world-class swimmers.

Swimming efficiency is about the discipline of hundreds of semi-isometric contractions of the involved muscles as the body slides past the hand seeking an elusive hold on the water. Over mile after mile of training, swimmers learn the gross-motor genius of just the right amount of pressure, along with disciplined skeletal posture allowing for the greatest horizontal velocity and the least amount of drag.

Swimming fast defies shortcuts; it is the only sport that takes place in a medium foreign to the one we live in daily. It is among the athletic world's purest forms of competition.

At no point in the sport of swimming does it matter where you were born, what school you attended, or how much wealth your grandparents may have accumulated. One hundred percent of the time, success is the direct result of the work a swimmer has done. At least that was true until the Montreal Olympics.

While the 1976 men's team was led by men who swam for the world's best swimming coaches in a fully developed NCAA swimming system dating back to the 1930s, women's collegiate swimming was in its infancy. Without the NCAA program for support post-high school, on the women's team only Karen, Shirley, Kim, and backstroker Melissa Belote were return competitors from Munich.

Upon their arrival in the athlete village in Montreal, the USA women and men were able to rally enough political capital to get three-time Olympian Gary Hall elected as flag bearer for the USA contingent in the opening-ceremony parade. It is hard to believe, given the rich history of the USA men's and women's swim teams, that Montreal remains the only Olympics in which a swimmer has carried the flag.

The Montreal Olympic Swimming Pool was state of the art.
(Photo credit: Swimming World Magazine)

With swimming events starting the day after the opening ceremonies, many of the women swimmers, including Shirley Babashoff, elected not to march in the parade of nations. Instead, Shirley took a day of rest in preparation for a week in which she was scheduled for an unprecedented eleven Olympic races.

Kornelia Ender and most of her teammates sat out the opening ceremonies as well. Ender recalls the wonder of the Olympic Village. They lounged in a riverside amphitheater and listened to a live concert by Canadian Gordon Lightfoot. The athlete dining hall was almost too much for the East Germans to comprehend. The bins of the cafeteria overflowed with freshly grilled T-bone steaks, roasted potatoes and fresh vegetables. It was Canadian blueberry season. Bowls of unreasonably large sweet purple berries were on the athlete's tables 24 hours a day.

Sunday, July 18, 1976

The women's swimming competition at Montreal began in relative obscurity with the preliminary heats of the 100 freestyle on the morning of Sunday, July 18. The swim stadium in Montreal was like nothing any of the athletes or coaches had ever seen. The pool itself was deep, a minimum of two meters. The interior walls of the building formed a modernistic oblong shape around the competition pool for bleachers that accommodated 10,000 fans.

Away from the television cameras and commentators, the coaches and swimmers must have experienced the first round of preliminary heats at Montreal much like any of the dozens of swim meets that had brought them to this point in their lives.

In the 100 freestyle heats, Shirley swimming the first of her eleven swims, went just fast enough to move on to the semi-finals. Ultimately, the 100 free would be her most uninspired swim of the Games. She would end up fifth in the finals on the following night. Her own analysis of the type of work she was doing at the West Point training camp seemed to be right on. Going into the Olympics, Shirley started out sluggish without the steady mix of distance and speed work she'd known over the previous three years with Mark Schubert.

By contrast, Kornelia Ender must have seemed unbeatable. Coming into the meet, she was the only woman in history to swim faster than 56 seconds in a 100 freestyle. While most of the competitors, including the women from the USA, swam just fast enough to move from prelims to semis and into the finals, Kornelia swam a 55 second 100 in the prelims and semis. From the start, she gave the impression that she had limitless reserves.

On Sunday night, the TV lights came on and the swim stadium was packed from floor to ceiling with fans. For the two heats of semi-finals, the reality of the Olympic Games must have come alive to the USA team. Kim Peyton went into the semis seeded second behind Kornelia with Jill Sterkel fourth. Kim won the first semi heat with an American Record, swimming almost a full second faster than her Olympic Trials time. Jill finished third in the heat just behind Kim and Enith Brigitha of Holland.

In the second semifinal heat, Shirley seemed to respond to

the big stage and the crowd, finding a way to swim fast. She finished second behind Kornelia and ahead of both Claudia Hempel and Petra Premier, East Germany's number two and three swimmers.

4x100-Medley Relay

Swim meets are like all athletic events, with shifts in momentum, and one of the coach's jobs is to manage the accompanying emotions. Jack Nelson would have been able to predict that the USA had a slim chance against the East Germans in the week of swimming that lay ahead, but the coach's ever-positive outlook may have dimmed a bit after the final of the medley relay. *Swimming World* recorded the first final of the Games by pointing out that "the [East German] women are so far superior in the medley relay that fine performances by other countries often go unnoticed. All eight countries making the finals improved their national record, with countries like the USSR dropping their standard by over 10 seconds." [65]

The super era of modern swimming knew no international borders as six out of the eight lead-off splits established new 100 backstroke records for their countries, including the USA's Linda Jezek, who improved her own American Record from the Olympic Trials.

In any other circumstances, the USA swimmers and coaches would likely have been very pleased with the first event of the meet. The USA team performed exactly how any national team with high expectations would have scripted it: with personal best times in every leg. Following Jezek's lead-off American Record in the backstroke, Lauri Siering's breaststroke split was 7/10 of a second faster than her time in June.

Prior to the medley relay the coaches must have discussed who should swim the fly and free legs. Wendy was training well and clearly on a steep trajectory of improvement based on her swims at Trials. Shirley was the top qualifier from the Trials, but Kim had broken Shirley's 100 free American Record in the semi heats. The coaches might have discussed Jill as well. She was the wildcard, a fifteen-year-old kid who appeared to have no end to her abilities and competitive drive. Coming off of three American short-course records at the exhibition meet in West Point and without the history of the Belgrade and Cali World Championships, she might have been the least intimidated by the East Germans. This must have given Jack Nelson and the other coaches pause to consider her for the anchor leg.

In the end Jack went with the top qualifiers out of the Trials—Camille Wright for the fly, Shirley for the free—and the few tenths of a second the USA might have gained would not have made any difference in the outcome. Camille split 1:00.64 to put the USA back in second place. Shirley closed with 56.11, beating her Trials time of 56.96. Even with a 6-second loss to the East Germans, the coaches must have come away from the medley relay with a bit of relief. The silver medal performance showed the USA women were swimming well, and Shirley was in a good place.

The experience of the USA men's team could not have been a greater contrast from the women's team. At the first team meal back in Los Angeles, Doc Counsilman in a moment of leadership genius had galvanized the focus of the male swimmers. "Gentlemen, this is the greatest Olympic team ever assembled. I believe this team, if you decide to come together and prepare, can win every gold medal in Montreal. And I believe you can sweep many of the events." [66]

On the first day of finals, three American men brought Counsilman's vision to life. Coming into the Games, East Germany's Roger Pytel held the 200 butterfly world record, In the first event of the meet for the USA men, Steve Gregg, a sophomore at North Carolina State University, went into the finals seeded first. Two other Americans, Bill Forrester and Mike Bruner, were also in the final. In a pre-race interview Steve Gregg laid out the USA's strategy: "We've seen Pytel swim this race many times. I think if we can stay close to him, all three Americans will swim by him in the last 50 meters." [67]

In a surprise for the reigning world record holder Roger Pytel, Bill Forrester, one of the youngest members of the USA team, led the first 100 meters swimming in the outside lane. True to Doc Counsilman's vision and Steve Gregg's prediction, Pytel's stroke shortened coming off the final turn and the three Americans buried him in the final 50 meters to sweep the first event of the Montreal Olympics.

After day one of the Montreal Games, the trajectory for the USA men and the East German women was set. And for Shirley and her teammates, the week's struggle against the steroid-enhanced performances of the East Germans had just begun.

Monday, July 19

The first two individual finals on the women's program at Montreal were the 200 fly and the 100 free. In the 100 Shirley, Kim, and Jill would face East Germany's best. The results, while fairly predictable at the top with Kornelia Ender's current world record more than a second ahead of Kim's new American Record, would serve as an assessment of the USA's chances in the freestyle relay the following Sunday.

100 Freestyle

Kornelia Ender's rise to dominance in the 100 freestyle had been astounding. She was the first woman ever to break 58 seconds in a 100 free, the first woman to break 57, and as she stood on the blocks in the Olympic final, she was the only woman on planet earth who had swum under 56 seconds.

Ender on top of the podium after the 100 freestyle with the Netherland's Enith Brigitha in the background.
(Photo credit: Swimming World Magazine)

Looking ahead to the 4x100-free relay with the USA seeded second, third, and sixth, the coaches must have had a glimmer of hope as they considered the girls' prospects. Kornelia Ender was clearly dominant, but the Americans were within reach of the other East Germans.

Olympic coaches have to be emotionally steady in the face of the highs and lows of a multi-day competition, but even Jack Nelson's unbridled positive outlook must have taken another beating as the USA swimmers finished out of the medals in the first individual event at Montreal. Kim lowered her own American Record from the semis again, finishing fourth just ahead of Shirley while Jill Sterkel ended up seventh. Suddenly, it seemed that even the most positive of outlooks would have to concede that the 4x100-free relay upset that Kim Peyton dreamed of at the Trials was unlikely.

The 100 freestyle was the first of many historic injustices brought on by East German doping. Enith Brigitha from Holland won the bronze medal, finishing behind East Germany's Kornelia Ender and Petra Premier. Without the performance enhancement of anabolic steroids, Enith Brigitha would have held the distinction of becoming the first swimmer of African descent to win an Olympic gold, breaking the race barrier in Olympic swimming. Instead, twelve years after Montreal, Suriname's Anthony Nesty was recognized as the first swimmer of African descent to become an Olympic champion in swimming, when he won the 100 butterfly at the 1988 Olympics in Seoul.

200 Butterfly

The USA women swimmers at Montreal were either high school age, or they were piecing together training and college at the dawn of Title IX. Karen Moe Thornton's path to Montreal was fairly typical of the women on the USA team, neither easy nor traditional as each had to forge her own way.

At Montreal, Karen was out at the 100 split more than a second faster than her American Record at the Trials. Would she have pushed the front end so hard if she were not chasing the East Germans? She finished only slightly ahead of Canada's Wendy Quirk. Both girls were strong back-half swimmers. But without the East Germans to chase, would Karen have laid up a bit in the front half of the swim assuming she could run Wendy Quirk down in the second 100? And would it have been enough, as Quirk swam only slightly slower than Karen did coming home?

In the end history will show that Karen Moe Thornton finished fourth at Montreal, in an American Record and more than 2.5 seconds faster than she swam when she won the gold in Munich in 1972. The East Germans swam to a 1-2-3 finish, sweeping the 200 butterfly.

None of the finals at Montreal can ever be swum again, and all of the intricacies of the races have been forever tainted by the coaches, doctors and leaders of East Germany.

The East German steroid use leaves so many questions never to be answered. The swimmers were obviously well coached. In a 1974 article esteemed Australian coach Forbes Carlisle observed the technical aspect of the East German national team as being among the best in a practice setting. [68] How would they have fared without the aid of steroids? Perhaps the team would have emerged in the '70s and '80s among the best in the world without the steroid pills and injections of testosterone. The program was based on good science, attention to detail, and sound training plans, mixed with overt cheating.

For Karen Moe Thornton, who went on to a pioneering

career among women's college coaches, the questions will never be answered. In a strange twist it could be argued that Karen, Shirley, and the next wave of USA women swimmers might never have been pushed to the level of swimming excellence they achieved without the East German doping program pressing them onward. Almost forty years after Montreal, Karen reflects on her Olympic career.

"I think of where my place in history would have been if I had been awarded the gold in Montreal. Very few people are back-to-back Olympic champions." [69]

Tuesday, July 20

400 Freestyle

With so many variables among individuals, the drama of every Olympic competition plays out in the unexpected. Swimmers who appear to be unstoppable sometimes have an off day, while long shots hit all the variables just right and explode into history as champions.

At the Montreal Games, the expectations for Shirley Babashoff were astronomical. In the first Olympics following Mark Spitz's epic domination of the Munich Games, there was talk of as many as seven gold medals for Shirley. Privately, no one in the swimming community expected seven golds. Kornelia Ender was more than a second ahead of the world in the 100 free, and the East German medley relay was a dream team, with each of the four swimmers current world record holders in their specialty events. But three golds, maybe four, if the free relay could find superhuman effort, seemed a real possibility for Shirley. In the highs and lows of the meet facing them, Shirley's performances could be the catalyst to help propel the team in face of East German domination.

"Shirley is a big psych-up for everybody else on the team. She's our leader. She'll pull us along with her," butterflier Camille Wright said after Babashoff's epic performance at the Trials. [70]

So it must have caused the USA coaches and especially Shirley Babashoff a moment of real hopefulness a few weeks before Montreal when the East Germans announced that their top distance swimmer, Barbara Krause, would not make the trip to the Olympics.

A month prior to Montreal, Krause had broken Shirley's world record in the 400 free at the East German Olympic

Trials. The matchup between the two of them in the 400 free was as anticipated as the 200-free matchup between Shirley and Kornelia.

In the years since the Berlin Wall fell and East Germany's state-run doping program was uncovered, it has never been made clear why Barbara stayed

East Germany's Petra Thürmer.
(Photo credit: Swimming World Magazine)

home from the Montreal Olympics. The story reported to the swimming press was that she was suffering from a throat infection. The *Los Angeles Times*[71] reported Krause was kept out of the competition because of "angina," while *Sports Illustrated* wrote that she did not make the trip because of "throat inflammation."[72]

Given the secrecy of the doping program and the suspicion among the swimming world, it is fair to speculate that a pre-competition test had shown traces of steroids in Barbara Krause's urine. Decades later a Canadian Broadcasting Corporation article marking the thirtieth anniversary of the Montreal Games confirms the suspicions: "Krause … was forced out of the 1976 Olympics because team doctors had miscalculated her dose of drugs and worried she might test positive at the Games."

The nation of East Germany was not about to have the suspicion of doping jeopardize the success they anticipated in Montreal should Barbara not pass the drug test. The cost would have been too great. Though she went on to star in the U.S.-boycotted Moscow Games in 1980, the sporting world, ironically, can add Barbara Krause to the list of victims of the doping program.

In the final of the 400 free, Shirley swam stroke for stroke with the East German's second-best distance swimmer, fifteen-year-old Petra Thümer. Both swam under Krause's world record, but in the final 100 Thümer pulled ahead to win the gold.

The astonishing acceleration of swim times made possible by the little plastic goggle extended through the '76 Games.

American male swimmer Don Schollander's winning time at the 1964 Games just twelve years earlier would have been good enough for only the bronze medal in the women's event in 1976. America's second and third male finishers from 1968, Roy Saari and the head coach of Shirley's Olympic team, Jack Nelson, would have had to settle for sixth and seventh in the women's 400 at Montreal. Even so, the 400 freestyle was the first of a series of near misses and disappointments for Shirley Babashoff.

Back in the dorms in the Olympic village, her teammates, sensing Shirley's disappointment, either went to bed before she got back to the dorms or left the apartment for a while so as not to have to face her.

Wednesday, July 21

At the Olympic level, it is hard to imagine that the outlook of an entire team could be contingent upon the success of any single individual, but after Shirley's 400 freestyle the previous night, Wednesday was undoubtedly a low point for the USA swimmers and coaches as not one of the women advanced to the finals. Midway through the meet, the dilemma for Jack Nelson was to look at the events remaining in the program and try to find a bright spot. A man programmed to look at every situation in the most positive light, it must have taken an extra measure of positivity for Jack to find much for the team to rally around.

100 Backstroke

The 100 backstroke marked the first time since 1952 that an American team had failed to have a swimmer qualify in the top eight for the finals at an Olympic Games. Linda Jezek, coming off of an American Record lead-off in the 400 medley, relay slipped on her start.

America's top 100-meter backstroke swimmer Linda Jezek set the American Record leading off the Medley Relay. *(Photo credit: Swimming World Magazine)*

In the same race, a historic achievement was stolen from the Canadians when fourteen-year-old Canadian swimmer Nancy Garapick finished third behind two East Germans in the 100 backstroke.

Not only would Garapick have presumably brought home gold and set the world record in the 100 back, she was followed by teammates Wendy Hogg and Cherly Gibson. The Canadians would have swept the medals.

200 Breaststroke

The surprise of the night and one of the biggest at Montreal was the shutout of the East Germans in the 200 breaststroke. They entered the meet with the current world record holder, as well as the 1975 World Champion. Their third swimmer, Carola Nitschke, came into the meet with the fastest time in the world in 1976. The 1-2-3 sweep of the USSR in the 200 breaststroke had to come as a shock to the East German team.

The winner, Marina Koshevaya, dropped an astounding 12.5 seconds over the course of the year to claim the gold medal. While this kind of improvement is not unprecedented in Olympic swimming, it is rare. However, nothing suggests that the USSR, even with its influence and relationship with East Germany, was involved in doping its swimmers at the 1976 Olympics.

The USA women, led by team captain Marcia Morey, finished fifteenth, sixteenth, and twenty-fifth in the 200 breaststroke.

Thursday, July 22
100 Fly

The following day, things brightened up for Jack Nelson and the other USA coaches when all three USA swimmers qualified for the finals of the 100 fly. However, the big story in the press was not the American swimmers; it was Kornelia Ender, who entered the evening's finals seeded first in the 100 fly and third in the 200 free. In the finals of the 100 fly Kornelia faced what *Swimming World* called "Chapter One of one of the greatest moments in Olympic swimming history." [73]

Up to that point in Olympic history, only one individual, Finnish distance runner Paavo Nurmi, had won two events in one night, turning in gold-medal performances in both the 1,500 and 5,000 meters at the 1924 Paris Olympics.

"Even greater than Mark Spitz," [74] gushed the swimming press, was Kornelia if she was successful in winning the gold in both races on Thursday.

Of the benefits of anabolic steroid use, two stand out in light of Kornelia's performance on the fifth night of finals in Montreal. One of the great benefits of steroids is an improved rate of recovery, which clearly helped her in between the races. However, winning two Olympic finals in one night goes beyond mere physical demands. It requires extreme confidence in oneself.

Ominously, it seems the nation of Germany had recognized the additional psychotropic benefit of steroid use as far back as World War II when frontline Nazi troops were said to have been administered anabolics to aid them in their aggressiveness. [75] Indeed, the first whispers of East German steroid use were accompanied by the observation that the women athletes in particular seemed to react with arrogance toward the women of other nations. [76]

In the 100 fly Kornelia Ender led from wall to wall; teammate Andrea Pollack followed in second. Wendy Boglioli's husband, Bernie, never saw the

Wendy Boglioli with her parents in Montreal.
(Photo credit: Wendy Boglioli)

second 50 of the 100 butterfly. At the turn he took note of Wendy's split and knew she was going to have the swim of her life. With tears in his eyes, he was overcome with emotion and had to sit down. Wendy finished in 1:01.17, the fastest time ever by a woman swimming without the performance enhancement of anabolic steroids.

The results show Wendy Boglioli finishing third in American Record time, just ahead of teammate Camille

Wright. What would have been a gold-silver performance by the Americans was lost in the deceit of a nation bent on prominence through sport. At any cost.

To date, the results of the Montreal Games have not been adjusted or even noted with an asterisk acknowledging the documented, systematic state-sponsored doping of women swimmers. Experts in the antidoping field speculate that one of the reasons for the International Olympic Committee's reluctance to rewrite the history of the Montreal Games is because the USA is seen historically as the biggest offender in anabolic steroid use. Swimming in the USA, for the most part has not been implicated in steroid doping, but at the 1983 Pan American Games in Caracas, Venezuela when it was discovered that new, more sophisticated doping tests were in place 12 American track and field athletes withdrew from competition.

200 Freestyle

The 200-free dual between Ender and Babashoff was much anticipated. In what may have been a surprise win the previous summer in the Cali World Championships, Shirley had passed Kornelia in the second 100. The race was always interesting because Kornelia was swimming "up" to the 200 as the world's best 100 freestyler and Shirley, while a very strong 100 freestyler, was, by the time of the Montreal Games, swimming "down" to the 200 as the best in the 400 and 800.

For years Shirley Babashoff's race strategy had been an open book. Everyone knew that she and her Animal Lane teammates trained to have great back-half swims. She would go out steady and fast, but set up to have a great second 100.

She planned, if not to negative split the 200, to be as close to even in her splits as possible. Shirley's ability to close a race had achieved a certain mythological status. No one in the world wanted to try to outswim her in the last 50 meters of any race.

The ability to press the front end of a race, to swim within herself, yet stay in touch with any competitor and then redline the heart-lung-muscle energy delivery system in the back half of a race was legendary. It was as though coach Mark Schubert had effectively spliced a functioning reserve into her DNA.

Not much escaped the attention of Kornelia's coaches. They recognized Shirley's race strategy and made calculated adjustments in Kornelia's training after her loss to Shirley the previous summer.

"I always used to take it out hard," Ender told the press after the Montreal 200. "At Cali, I started too fast and couldn't hold it. For more than a year, I've trained to stay with Shirley at the 100 and have more coming home."[77]

Much was made of the 26-minute rest interval between the 100 fly and the 200 free. In the interim, Kornelia swam easy in the warm down pool, tried to relax, and made a trip to the podium to receive her gold medal for the 100 fly.

In the 200-free final, Kornelia was off the blocks first, and the two swimmers swam even for 150 meters. The last 50 was not the match-up most people anticipated as Kornelia swam away from Shirley. Mark Schubert described the last 50 as the "tipping point" for him. Shirley could have and should have won that race he said, but Kornelia out-split Shirley in the last 50 by almost 2 full seconds. Schubert had seen Shirley drop into a lower gear and beat the best swimmers in the world in just the same manner for the past four years. At the point where Ender picked up her kick and left Shirley in her wake, the immense advantage of the steroid program took on a new clarity for Mark Schubert.

Kornelia Ender's year-long training strategy, aided by the physical and psychotropic benefits of the anabolic steroids, resulted in her second gold medal of the night and her fourth world record at the Games.

Friday, July 23

The swimmers had Friday off, which was good for Shirley. She had finally come unglued at the press conference following the 200 freestyle.

"Personally, I don't think the East Germans enjoy swimming. It seems the East Germans are very restricted. We play around in the water. They think about working hard and nothing else," Shirley told the International Press. [78]

Joe Gergen from *Newsday* remembers she came off snotty. He would characterize Shirley as spoiled and "mocking the Olympic spirit." [79] Gergen says he was reacting to a week-long buildup of behaviors, from Shirley not congratulating Petra Thümer after the 400 freestyle to making fun of the East Germans on a bus ride to the training pool. Accustomed to covering professional sports teams in New York City, Gergen was covering his first Olympics in 1976. His expectations of Olympic athletes were those of finding the athletic purists, the amateurs, those who competed for love of the sport, not for a paycheck. In his reports from Montreal, Gergen lumped the entire USA women's team in with Shirley.

"[Y]ou always think there is a certain amount of honor in the Olympics. You'd like to think so.... And they did react spoiled because they didn't satisfy themselves," he concluded. [80]

The disappointment of consecutive second-place finishes in light of the enormous expectations coming into the Olympics had begun to catch up with the USA's top swimmer and team leader. Later in the week, Shirley would go toe-to-toe with a reporter who asked her if she was disappointed with another silver medal.

"How many silver medals do you have at home?" she retorted. [81] In a demonstration of the fact that the pen is mightier than the sword, the press schooled around her like hungry sharks. From *Swimming World* to *Newsday* and *The New York Times*, Shirley was roundly criticized as a bad sport.

With two days of swim competition left, head coach Jack Nelson's team dynamics problem seemed to go from bad to worse. Some of the swimmers who were done swimming their events began to ignore curfew. The party had started for many of the athletes in the historic district of Old Montreal where complimentary champagne flowed. Team Manager Carol Finneran tried her best to keep order but somehow missed the mark again, waking and accusing innocent swimmers of blowing the curfew while others went unchallenged.

Chapter 13

JACK ROLLS THE DICE

ON FRIDAY WITH THE BREAK in the swimming events, the coaches took the opportunity to shift the focus of attention from the past week of competition to the 4x100-free relay, the one event they still held out hope for. The relay team took the short bus ride to the auxiliary pool to practice starts. With a historic rout underway at the hands of the East Germans, Jack Nelson must have wondered if he had enough credibility left with the team to actually influence the women on the relay. But it was Nelson's very nature to be bold.

Kornelia Ender and Kim Peyton at the finish of the 100 freestyle final.
(Photo credit: Swimming World Magazine)

In interviews decades after Montreal, he tells the story better than anyone, his voice rising with emotion. "They always swim Ender first," he said to the girls. He spoke to Kim Peyton but he would have picked a moment when he was sure that Shirley was listening.

"Probably those big German egos. They want her out first for another world record split. You don't have to beat her, Kim. Just chase her like a bulldog. Don't let her get away." [82]

The women on the USA team had underestimated the coach, missing a key element of the man's character that set him apart among his peers. Perhaps it went hand in hand with all the overt cheerfulness and gleeful positivity the man projected; Jack Nelson was a risk taker. Along with that, he was a keen observer of the world and especially of the athletes he accepted responsibility for.

With the opportunity to speak confidence into their lives at hand, Nelson's risk-taking intuition took over and he leapt upon the opportunity to deliver the message. For all the miscues since the team had assembled, the coach, for possibly the first time, was completely clear and right on the mark. The arithmetic of the splits gave the girls a fighting chance. The missing ingredient was belief.

After a week of being demolished by the East Germans, along with the beating they'd taken outside of the pool at the hands of press, these women needed to believe. Jack Nelson, the self-made, strong-mind-strong-performance coach, was perhaps the one person on earth uniquely equipped for the moment.

Jill Sterkel, just fifteen years old, was a sponge. With confidence in her skill and her competitive nature, she was ready to accept any direction. Wendy was raised to believe in her coaches. If her coach, Bill Palmer, trusted Nelson, then Wendy would trust Nelson. The soul of the team was Kim—every member of the team loved Kim, even Shirley.

Shirley, though, was the toughest to reach, and the one most in need of hope. In his wisdom Nelson reached her through Kim Peyton. His gravelly voice dropped to a conversational tone, a near whisper for him.

"You don't have to beat her, Kim," he repeated. "Just have to chase her down the pool so hard she'll wish she'd never met you." Here he was bold. Kim and Shirley were the most veteran swimmers on the team. The two of them had born much of the burden of keeping the USA close to the East Germans between Munich and Montreal; even so, Kim had lived to some degree in Shirley's shadow.

"Kim," said Nelson, placing the race squarely on her shoulders, "you are the key. You are going to keep us close enough to give us a chance."

As he spoke to each girl, Jack communicated some masterful magic beyond the words—the message of a good coach with their best interest at heart, a coach who believed in them.

"Wendy, you're going to go second. Your job is to close the gap."

"Jill, you are going to get us the lead." He paused to let the image of the USA team in the lead take hold.

Shirley, with all her international experience, allowed Jack Nelson to coach her for perhaps the first time. His message was matter of fact: "Shirley, no one can beat you when you have the lead."

"One more thing," he said to the whole group. "When you four are in the ready room, I want ya'll to be happy, not too solemn. This team knows what it's about. Have some fun in there." [83]

Message delivered. Message absorbed. Jack Nelson, the smiling sideshow man, released the women like a magician releasing white doves from the empty palms of his hands.

On the bus to the pool, assistant coach Jim Montrella fretted. He and Frank Elm had discussed other possibilities for the relay. Maybe Shirley should swim first, let the frustration of four silver-medal finishes fuel a swim that was over her head. But he kept these thoughts to himself. In his wisdom, Montrella let Nelson's vision rule the day, and they spent an hour rehearsing race-speed finishes and relay starts in the order the head coach had described.

After the relay practice session, Kim Peyton, the girl fond of braiding her hair in two long pig tails and wearing a hippy-esque headband, found a way to both lighten the mood of her teammates and help them refocus. The girls bought Olympic suspenders to wear on the podium, and they made a visit to the music lounge at the Olympic Village where Jill, Shirley, and Kim made a karaoke tape version of the Eagles' "Take it to the Limit." Jill remembers the recorded tape version as being "pretty terrible," but fun. [84] Of course none of them knew any of the words, only the chorus and the critical message of taking it to the limit "one more time." Shirley and her teammates needed this moment to be kids again, to laugh and remember to enjoy the moment. Somehow, intuitively, Kim Peyton helped her teammates embrace the joy of competing in the pressure cooker of the Olympic Games.

In the day and a half remaining before the relay, the other thing the four swimmers did in preparation was to revisit the mental imagery training they'd received before the '75 World Championships.

They focused attention inward, visualized themselves swimming the relay, watched themselves achieve the split times needed for an upset of the East Germans in each of their individual legs. [85] Sterkel and Boglioli also took time to pray before the relay. The task before them would require their best efforts and maybe a little assistance from the Almighty.

Saturday, July 24

In perhaps the most controversial move of the Games for the USA, Jack Nelson in consultation with Mark Schubert, who up to this point had mostly stayed out of the USA coach's business, scratched Shirley from the 400 IM. At this point, Shirley needed some rest. She could cruise the preliminary heats of the 800 free, but adding a prelim and final of the 400 IM could be disastrous. Shirley's IM at the Olympic Trials, even with improvement, would have been a long shot for a medal, much less a gold.

If the meet had been going differently, if Shirley had been competing on a level playing field with three gold medals in hand and all the confidence in the world, she might have swum the 400 IM. Given both Mark Schubert's and Shirley Babashoff's competitive natures, it is a good bet that she would have. But we will never know. Under the circumstances, swimming the IM made no sense.

400 IM

In another injustice to the host nation, the Canadians were denied an Olympic gold and silver finish for Cheryl Gibson and Becky Smith. East Germany's Ulrike Tauber swam an astounding 6 seconds under the existing world record to win the gold. In hindsight the world knows now that Canadian Cheryl Gibson swam the fastest non-anabolic steroid enhanced 400 IM in Montreal. But Olympic history to date has never been amended. The record shows silver for Gibson and bronze for her Canadian teammate, Becky Smith.

100 Breaststroke

The USA team suffered another setback when none of its swimmers advanced to the finals for the third time at the Games. The USSR finished second and third behind Hannelore Anke from East Germany, denying the Russian athletes a sweep of the breaststroke events.

Sunday, July 25

On the last day of the Games, Canadian swimmer Nancy Garapick may have vindicated the mayor of Montreal, the man who had the vision to bring the Games to Canada. The fourteen-year-old had already won a bronze medal earlier in the week.

200 Backstroke

Again, Nancy Garapick took a third-place finish in the 200 backstroke behind the East German swimmers. Even so, *Swimming World* reported that "the gold medals, the [East German] women, the world, and Olympic records—they were all secondary to the Canadian's performance."

The partisan Canadian fans, who filled the 9,200-capacity Olympic Park pool, seemed happier for the little fourteen-year-old from Nova Scotia winning her second bronze medal. Nancy was the Canadian hero of the Games to that point.

"I got one telegram from Halifax," she said, "which was about twenty-five feet long. It feels okay to represent your country and win two medals." [86]

It is hard to imagine the sense of pride that would have swept the city and the nation had the Canadian women swimmers brought home the three golds, six silvers, and three bronze medals they deserved but were denied by the East German doping program.

The host nation, which had invested heavily in facilities and coaching personnel in the four-year lead-up to the Games, would have enjoyed the most successful Olympics in its history.

800 Freestyle

Shirley had one more chance. The 800 freestyle was likely her best shot at an individual gold medal. For almost nine minutes she swam stroke for stroke with East Germany's Petra Thümer in a replay of their 400 freestyle battle. In the end she swam two seconds under her own pending world record—and was touched out by four tenths of a second.

In the final tally at Montreal only three USA women swimmers would come home with individual medals from the '76 Games. Shirley with her ever-growing collection of silver medals, Wendy Boglioli's bronze in the 100 fly and the USA's Wendy Weinberg who finished 3rd in the 800 freestyle behind Thümer and Babashoff.

In the post-race interview, Shirley was even more defensive than she'd been after the 400 free. The press now seemed determined to portray her as a sore loser.

"Every event I swim I try to win."

"No, I'm not frustrated. I feel great. I've done really great times—my 100 was my best, my 200 was my second best, my 400 was my best by a long ways, and our medley relay did really well."

The press seemed insistent that she had failed in achieving her goals. How could her swims be labeled a success?

"What do you mean by success?" she replied. "Isn't second place good? I've done my best times and that's what I'm here for.""" [87]

With the 4x100-free relay left to swim in a long and disappointing week, Shirley Babashoff and the rest of the USA women faced a hostile press and an East German team riding high on confidence and anabolic steroids.

Chapter 14

THE GREAT RACE

BEFORE THE 4x100-RELAY RACE, the faces of the USA girls are focused. Gone is Shirley's great gaping yawn as seen before her world record in the 800 at the Olympic Trials in Long Beach. Determined and workman-like perhaps best describes the relay team behind the starting blocks.

They pace. They talk without looking at one another. They know each other; superficialities are needless. They don't look desperate or defeated. They might be a group of climbers assembling at base camp for the final assault on the summit. A group with a great task before them. There is a hint of hope in their demeanor, something in the small talk, the tugging at suit hems, the pacing, says they believe they just might have a

Shirley Babashoff would anchor the 4x100 freestyle relay for the USA.
(Photo credit: Swimming World Magazine)

chance. Shirley, the superstar, stands next to 15-year-old Jill. Shirley says something, looking off toward the far end of the pool. Jill says nothing, just listens, and fidgets with her suit. She shakes out an arm.

Kornelia Ender leans over rapidly stroking her freestyle arm movements in the air. She is prepared to do her part but does not take anything for granted. Even with the total domination over the USA during the previous week of swimming, no one on the East German team seems to take anything for granted. The East German women are great competitors, seasoned over the years between Munich and Montreal. They are unaware at the moment, that fifteen years hence, history will show that they have been pawns in the hands of the state. They are the crowning glory of State Planning Theme 14.25.

At Munich four years earlier, the East German team had set the world record in the 4x100-free relay in the prelims only to be touched out by the USA in the finals. They are not about to leave anything to chance in this final showdown with the USA. East German strategy since the Belgrade World Championships is to lead off with Kornelia Ender.

Maybe it's pride, maybe it is a bit of arrogance among the coaches who desire another world record performance, or maybe it's strategy—deliver a crushing blow to any American dreams of an upset. Clearly, if Ender just swims her best, she will set up her team with what may well be an insurmountable lead. Following Kornelia will be Petra Premier, the silver medalist in the 100 free. Andrea Pollack, the gold medalist in the 200 fly, goes third. The East Germans will anchor with Claudia Hempel, who finished sixth, just ahead of Jill Sterkel, in the 100 free.

Based on the previous week of swimming it is clear the Americans are out of their league. East Germany starts the relay with the two fastest 100 freestyle swimmers in the world. It is hard to find a weak link in their squad. Is their slow swimmer the 200 butterfly gold medalist? Or the woman who out-touched Jill Sterkel in the 100 freestyle final?

USA assistant coach Jim Montrella remembers the East German political officer pacing at the warm up pool in Montreal before the relay. "I don't know exactly what her role was with the coaching staff, but she was clearly upset, and it had to do with the fourth swimmer, the anchor leg." [88]

It's not clear what the issue might have been with Claudia Hempel. With a team that includes two gold medalists and a silver medalist, it would seem that Claudia Hempel would need to simply hold her own to assure another East German victory. Maybe in the back of their minds the East German political handler and the coaches are remembering that they have left Barbara Krause, the second fastest 100 freestyler in the world, at home.

At the starting horn, Kornelia is off first as usual. Whatever the strategic thinking among the East German staff, Kornelia swims a precision driven 100 free for her team, touching the wall just over her own world record. Kornelia delivers for her teammates and for the "state," as she refers to her country in post-Olympic interviews.

"I gave the state quite a lot with my four gold medals," [89] she later says when asked about her plans to attend coveted medical doctor training after the Games. With the final event in the water, State Planning Theme 14.25 has succeeded beyond anyone's wildest imagination. Up to this point in Montreal, the East German women had won every gold medal but one.

By now the television commentators are big fans. ABC's Curt Gowdy introduces the event by describing the East German women swimmers as amazing. Commentator Donna de Varona, part of the 1964 Olympic champion relay team for the USA, predicts what everyone in the world assumes, that the East Germans will win the 4x100-free relay with ease. [90]

The swimmers on both teams emerge with one thing in common: consistent, Olympic freestyle strokes honed through years of repetition and racing. State Planning Theme 14.25 cannot produce this level of skill; only endless repetition in preparation for this moment can do it. The German and American swimmers have paid a heavy price to reach this level of mastery in their sport.

The USA swimmers' styles are in some ways consistent with their personalities. Kim is a torrent of tempo and attitude, not to be denied or intimidated. Wendy is refined, steady, and determined. Jill is power, like a three-year-old thoroughbred at the Kentucky Derby. Shirley is a Porsche winding up in third or fourth gear, the tachometer at its limit—any faster and the engine blows; any slower and the race is not won.

In the first leg, Kim does exactly what Jack Nelson asked of her. She trails Kornelia, holding an astounding .80 stroke tempo for the entire 100 meters. Most important, she refuses to acquiesce to the withering psychology of swimming in second place. She sets up her team so that they have a chance. Peyton trails Kornelia from wall to wall like a furious terrier never slowing even as Ender pulls steadily away by inches.

Kornelia Ender finishes her steroid-tainted Olympics with another dominating 100-freestyle performance on the relay. It will be decades later, after the doping program is revealed, when the world comes to realize that it was the drugs that for a time helped make her the top swimmer in the world. But for the moment, with her team leading by more than a second and Petra Premier, the 100-freestyle silver medalist in the water, it appears Ender's historic five-for-five gold medal performance is assured.

Wendy swims her leg just as Jack scripted. Her stroke is the most classic style among the USA swimmers, a model of freestyle from the pages of Doc Counsilman's textbook: precision with by far the most distance per arm stroke of any of her competitors. She swims over her head, the fastest 100 freestyle of her life, and closes to within a half second on Petra Premier.

Coach Jim Montrella's insistence on practicing the relay exchanges earlier in the week pays off as Jill's start is reasonably well-timed and executed. Sterkel swims as though she has been at a different meet for the past eight days. Evidently, no one told her that the East German girl should beat her.

With Sterkel closing fast on Andrea Pollack in the first 50 meters, the East German coaches must have begun to worry. They would know that Jill had qualified for the Olympic team in the 200 free, but that her best event was the 100. They may have hoped for Jill to fade, but the Germans know she has enough endurance to be among the best in the world in the 200. She comes out of the turn even with Pollack. Off the wall eight or ten strokes, Sterkel accelerates. She is gone. With the adrenaline of the moment, she pulls ahead little by little with each stroke.

The roar of the crowd at 65 meters when Sterkel takes over the race draws in announcer Curt Gowdy. A man with the experience of decades covering all of the biggest sporting events is overcome by the fierce courage of fifteen-year-old Jill Sterkel. Hope has appeared for the USA when least expected.

Shirley's relay start is sharp for once. Later, the East Germans would imply it had been a very good start. By today's standards, it would be considered well-timed. But for Shirley it shows where her mind is.

Babashoff was famous for not knowing a thing about the people she raced and generally beat. If they were fast enough to swim with her so be it, but she was the ultimate competitor, nothing would be surrendered without a struggle. Whether Shirley knew Claudia Hempel, the East German's anchor leg, or not, the USA coaches did. They'd dreamed of this scenario, crazy unconscious splits from the other three in order to put Shirley in a position to steal the win. The negative-split training made her back-half speed second nature. Stretching all the way back to the 1971 All Star Meet against the fledgling East German program, only one swimmer from another nation had ever come from behind to beat Shirley—Kornelia Ender.

The race was unfolding just the way coach Jack Nelson had envisioned it. Impossible to beat when she has the lead, Shirley enters the pool 4/10 of a second ahead of Hempel. She practically skips along the surface off her shallow start. Her high elbow recovery winds up to an astounding .91 stroke tempo in the first length. There is an urgency in her steady drumming two-beat kick not seen in the longer events. At the 50- meter mark, she turns ahead. Skidding again at the surface off the turn and climbing right back in to her spinning tempo.

Could any swimmer in the world catch her at this point? Could Ender have done it? Years of training with the boys in the Animal Lane, chasing them across 800-meter repeats, had toughened Shirley for this moment.

At some point she may have noticed the crowd noise. Curt Gowdy had never seen anything like it at a World Series or Super Bowl, where the efforts that define history often take place in the crack of the bat or sprint to the goal line. The steady building roar of the crowd in the swim stadium was something different altogether.

Somewhere Gene and Barb Peyton are in the crowd. Up high in the stands are Jill's mom, Joanne, and her dad, Jim, with his video camera. Wendy's mom and dad had surprised her, arriving in Montreal just in time for the relay. And standing along with the swimmers and coaches of the USA team, Mark Schubert is pulling at the hair at the nape of his neck. Wendy's husband, Bernie, the former swimmer turned coach, could see the upset unfolding.

Jack Nelson may have started breathing again, and the USA coaches may have let the hope bottled up inside them escape just a little. Gowdy calls the race for the USA with 20 meters to go.

Nelson had believed in a miracle, had willed the girls on the team to believe. The relay would be a defining event in the man's career; history would record Jack Nelson as a coach in his finest moment. Years later he would deflect the praise insisting, "The girls won with their minds."

Now he is swept up in the moment as the realization passes through the crowd. Perhaps Mark Schubert had known a bit earlier than most. Somewhere in the second 50 he may have noticed Shirley lock onto the East German swimmer's eyes, noticed the slight head waggle and surge in stroke that he'd seen for the past four years in countless workouts and competitions. With 10 meters to go, the Montreal swim stadium is a single roaring sound.

Shirley's trailing arm is stretched upward even as her other hand touches the wall. The wave following along behind her sweeps her toward the wall as she pumps her arm in the air in victory. On the deck is pure joy. Wendy has found her glasses so she can see the scoreboard at the far end of the pool. Kim, Wendy, and Jill embrace, hopping for joy like schoolgirls.

"At that point in the Olympics, everyone in the building wanted the USA to win that relay," Mark Schubert remembers. "I was standing with the US team during the race. At the finish it was unbelievable. People hugging everyone around them. If there had been high-fives back then, they would have been going on all over the place."

On the deck, the Canadians, the Dutch, the swimmers from all the other teams come to congratulate the USA women. Enith Brigitha gives Shirley a kiss on the cheek. There is a sense that this victory is a victory for all of them—for all the athletes who came to Montreal and competed in good faith.

[L to R] Shirley, Jill, Wendy, and Kim after the 4x100 freestyle relay. *(Photo credit: USA Swimming)*

Chapter 15

AFTER THE WALL

IN 1986 DR. LOTHAR KIPKE was invited to address the American Swim Coaches Association annual convention on the subject of East Germany's program of "Sport Medical Diagnostics."[91] As if the doping saga needed an appropriately named villain, the East German swimmers remember Lothar Kipke as one of the most reprehensible characters in their world. Even the Stasi, the East German secret police force, a group not known for empathy, had concerns about Kipke. He was particularly brutal, one Stasi report noted, in his administration of testosterone injections.[92]

After dazzling the American coaches with slides and data chronicling East Germany's methodical analysis of training loads and recovery by way of oxygen uptake, lactate millimoles and the speed of nitrogen elimination from the body, Kipke is roundly applauded. The fact that Dr. John Troup, who was the director of sports science for USA Swimming, invited Dr. Kipke to make a presentation at all speaks to the naivety of the leadership in USA Swimming and in the scientific community as well.

If East German athletes were "sport soldiers"—as Kornelia Ender, Petra Thümer, and Ines Geipel observed—then Dr. Kipke was the "sport general" in this war for East German superiority, and he would provide no useful information to the "enemy." The system in Communist Germany was set up to reward those who prevailed against the West. Helping the USA improve their program would not have served Dr. Kipke's personal and professional interests. In all the data and facts Dr. Kipke presented to the American coaches, the key element he failed to mention, of course, was the "supporting means." The extraordinary physiological effects of male hormones upon the performance of teenage women swimmers were expertly veiled from the American coaches.

The deception that had tainted Olympic sport for more than a decade might have continued indefinitely had it not been for the cataclysmic collapse of Eastern Bloc Socialist/Communist governments just three years after Dr. Kipke's talk. In November of 1989, life in East Germany changed overnight with the abrupt dismantling of the Berlin Wall. And the East German sport machine fell just as dramatically.

Ironically, the Montreal Olympics were the first where the International Olympic Committee (IOC) included anabolic steroids on the list of banned substances. The head of the IOC medical commission reported that the technology would be able to detect if an athlete had ingested steroids within two weeks of the competition. Three athletes of the more than 6,000 who competed in Montreal were disqualified because of steroid use. The three careless, or unlucky enough to be caught, were two weightlifters—one from the USA and one from Czechoslovakia—and a female discus thrower from Poland.[93]

The East German steroid of choice, Oral Turinabol, however, was invisible to the anti-doping technology. Steroid testing at Montreal was only able to detect a steroid if a sample of the exact compound for which they were testing was available. Because the state-run pharmaceutical company Jenapharm was the exclusive producer of Oral Turinabol, no sample was available outside of East Germany. In addition the technology in 1976 was not advanced enough to recognize injectable testosterone. East German doctors used testosterone as a bridging therapy to help sustain the effects of anabolics after athletes stopped using steroids in advance of competition.[94]

For anti-doping crusaders Brigitte Berendonk and Dr. Werner Franke, the participation of the medical community is what made doping in East Germany unconscionable. Berendonk and Franke were parents themselves. Early on in their marriage, knowing what they knew and still involved in international sport, they discussed if they would be able to recommend high-level sport to their own children when the time came. Ultimately, they believed they must challenge the steroid poisoning of young people in East Germany.

Husband and wife, Werner Franke and Brigitte Berendonk, waged a lifelong battle to expose State-sponsored doping of East German athletes. *(Photo credit: USA Swimming)*

The fight was not an easy one. The husband-and-wife team would be ostracized in their own athletic community. Upon the German publication of Berendonk's book, *Doping Dokumente*, they moved their family to Israel for a cooling-off period, reasoning that Israel was the safest place in the world for their family because of incredibly tight border security. Ultimately, Berendonk was sued in a French court where the judge ruled against her but levied a fine of only one franc in a testament to the rightness of her cause.

In a scene that might be taken from a Hollywood film, Dr. Franke and Berendonk, acting on a tip from colleagues, flew to the Medical Academy of the People's Army at Bad Saarow around Christmastime—just after the Berlin Wall came down and Germany reunified. Upon their arrival Dr. Franke notes that paper shredders at the former East German military hospital "were running hot."

With a letter from a West German army doctor colleague authorizing access to the facility, Franke was able to retrieve extensive documentation that revealed in great detail the doping program. The couple was able to save everything from doctoral theses, detailing both the positive and negative effects of anabolic steroid doping in athletes, to pages upon pages of meticulous handwritten notations. Berendonk characterized the recorded names, dates, dosages, and results of the East German doping program as "very German" in its detail. [95]

DOH Chairman and writer Ines Geipel marvels at the courage and resilience of Franke and Berendonk. "What I find special about him," she says of Dr. Franke's decades-long campaign on behalf of the victims, "is that he does everything out of love so that the person can deal with their own history."

Of Franke and Berendonk, Geipel notes that the two of them see the doping program, the necessity of the nation of East Germany to shine again through international sport, as a response to the "shame" endured by post-war Germans.

"Both of them" she says, "never stop thinking about German history." In their role as parents, former athletes and especially for Werner Franke as a man of science, the two "formulated a measurement," as Geipel puts it. The couple, fully aware of what was going on behind the veil of secrecy in East Germany, drew a proverbial line in the sand, saying in Geipel's view, simply, "One moment, this is criminal."[96]

So corrupt was this scientific community that East German scholars wrote doctoral dissertations on the best ways to schedule the training and doping of athletes to achieve optimal performance. In essence, they employed the integrity of academic inquiry to examine the very best ways to cheat.[97]

For Dr. Franke, this was intolerable. "I'm seeing this as the abuse of science. Not just the sports aspect.... The compounds, measurements, etc. that have been created in science for medical purposes, for patients ... They are being abused.

"For me giving drugs for no real reason, no [medically] acceptable reason, that is criminal behavior. ... [T]he abuse of science should be fought against by the scientists because they will be the only people who recognize this early enough," Dr. Franke concludes in a prophetic word to future generations.

Werner Franke, a descendent, he says, of the Westphalians who turned back the Roman Empire on their march into his native homeland, is clear in his own responsibility as a man

of science over the decades of the couple's battle to protect
athletes from the excesses that sport can motivate.

At Bad Saarow a former East German army officer con-
fronted Franke and Berendonk as they attempted to retrieve
evidence. "Never has a civilian been allowed to remove such
documents," insisted the officer. Franke, with little to stand
on but his own sense of moral authority and Westphalian
stubbornness, turned back the objection replying, "Never in
history has an army so completely capitulated as your East
German army has just done." [98]

It was not until the plane was in the air toward home, with
the doping documents in hand, that Berendonk and Franke
burst into relieved laughter, astonished at the surreal drama
that had just played out. [99] Truth be told, without this singular
act of courage, the doping story would likely still be a hazy set
of accusations.

Chapter 16

THE NEXT WAVE

DIRECTLY AFTER THE MONTREAL GAMES in 1976, coach George Haines delivers an after-action talk to American swim coaches. Entitled "Post-Olympic Evaluation of Olympic Swimming," Haine's talk exemplifies the confusion that would continue through the next decade. He had spent hours observing the East German women in Montreal. At the beginning of his talk, he says he believes that none of the East German swimmers were on steroids. In testament to the uncertainty among the swimming leadership, Haines concludes his talk by reversing his earlier position and asserting that a few of the East German women may have been using steroids. [100]

Haines is apologetic. The dismal showing of the USA women at Montreal is in part his fault and the fault of everyone in the room, he says to the coaches assembled. It's not the athletes' fault, nor Jack Nelson's fault. Whether or not the East Germans are using steroids, Haines says, cannot be used as a crutch. The system within the USA must provide the same opportunities to women as it does to men. He rallies the coaches to provide better competitive opportunities for women at both the high school and university level.

In fact, George Haines hardly mentions the men's team except to contrast their opportunities with what the women

have. The men, he notes, are toughened for international competition in the NCAA system of rivalry-fueled dual meets
between universities and an NCAA Championship that is the
most competitive swim meet in the world year-in and year-
out.

He rallies the coaches with a vision for how to make the
nation's women's programs stronger at every level—strength
training being a key element that must be incorporated
into the training program of young women. Indeed, Karen
Moe Thornton, Wendy Boglioli, and Jill Sterkel had all been
focusing on out-of-water strength training in their development prior to Montreal. This trend would progress years
later into a culture of strength and toughness among women
swimmers through dry-land training that prevails to this day.

John Leonard, who in 1985 would become the executive
director of the American Swim Coaches Association, remembers being a young coach with athletes on the national
team, listening from the back of the room while the eminent
coaches of the day argued the situation.

"Some of the younger coaches just felt like this was the
hand they were dealt and they would do their best to help the
young women they were coaching to compete against the East
Germans." [101]

The top coaches were in a real dilemma. They did not want
to send the message to their own swimmers that they were at
an unfair disadvantage and without a chance to win. They also
faced the reality that, without proof, their accusations about
the East Germans would probably come across as sour grapes.
No unified approach came out of the closed-door meetings,

but without question, the group in favor of silence prevailed.

In the years between Montreal in 1976 and Seoul in 1988, Mark Schubert continued to push the envelope with his team in Mission Viejo, and a new cadre of young coaches joined him, determined to find a way to compete at the international level, regardless of the specter of doping.

In a sense, George Haines' talk after Montreal would help galvanize the prevailing approach to competing with the East Germans through the '88 Olympics in Seoul. In response, a new wave of brilliant young American swimmers quickly appeared. Two years after Montreal, at the Third World Championships in West Berlin, the Americans were back on top. Tracy Caulkins, Joan Pennington, Nancy Hogshead, Cynthia "Sippy" Woodhead, and Kim Linehan joined forces with '76 veterans Jill Sterkel and backstroker Linda Jezek to resurrect USA prominence by winning nine out of thirteen events.

Tracy Caulkins and Joan Pennington were coached at the Nashville Aquatic Club by Paul Bergen. Bergen's temperament was much like Mark Schubert's, and he got results. He was a ruthless taskmaster. One of his assistant coaches at the time, Jay Fitzgerald, remembers a Saturday morning practice when Bergen summarily kicked both Tracy and Joan off the team for not executing their butterfly turn as he had taught them. The two arrived at the screen door of Bergen's house the next morning to ask for another chance to be on the team. They would, they assured Bergen, perform the butterfly turn exactly as he required from that point on.

Tracy's first world record came as a surprise at a run-of-the-mill regional meet. Her only rest in preparation for the meet was the van ride between Nashville and the pool at the University of South Carolina. [102]

One of the other newcomers, Sippy Woodhead, from Riverside, California, would have a Shirley Babashoff-like performance at the 1978 Summer Nationals where she would qualify for the World Championships in every freestyle event from the 100 to the 800. And Kim Linehan from the Sarasota YMCA would be the first USA swimmer since Shirley to regain the world record in the 400 freestyle.

For a moment with the momentum and confidence of the Berlin World Championships, the USA was poised to reassert its Olympic prominence at the 1980 Games in Moscow. And then came the USA boycott of those Games. When President Jimmy Carter announced that the USA would not compete in Moscow in response to the Soviet Union's invasion of Afghanistan, it dealt a tremendous blow to the USA women who were a just regaining their footing. Jill, Sippy, Tracy, as well as butterfly phenom Mary T Meagher, young swimmers at the height of their careers, suddenly had no Olympics to compete in—the ultimate swimming competition denied them by political forces at a global level.

By 1982, the damage of the 1980 boycott to the USA team was evident. Mark Schubert was head coach of the USA squad at Guayaquil, Ecuador, where the East Germans handed the USA a beating reminiscent of the '73 World Championships in Belgrade. The Germans won ten of fourteen events, while the USA could muster only two wins in the entire meet.

The USA was behind again in the run-up to the 1984 Games. Then came another political intrusion. In response to the 1980 USA boycott, East Germany joined the USSR and other Eastern Bloc nations in boycotting the Olympics in Los Angeles. The result in '84 was a best-of-the-West, hometown Olympics for the USA and its allies, complete with lots of gold medals and the stars of Hollywood.

A full twelve years—three Olympic quadrennial cycles—passed before all the world swimming powers came together again in Seoul, South Korea, for the 1988 Olympics. And the USA's unofficial policy of silence on the matter of doping was still in play.

Perhaps the USA's enthusiasm for speaking up on illegal performance enhancing drug use in Seoul was tempered by the positive drug test and subsequent removal of their top sprinter, Angel Myers, from the USA roster. In one of the most embarrassing moments in the history of USA Swimming, Myers' urine sample came back positive for the steroid Nandrolone. Ironically, Myer's disqualification led to Jill Sterkel, who'd missed the team by a few hundredths of a second, being added as a replacement for Myers in the 50 free.

At any point at the '88 Games, Mark Schubert or coach Richard Quick, who in later years would be a vocal critic of doping outbreaks in other countries, both of whom were on the '88 USA coaching staff, could have spoken out about their suspicions of the East Germans. Even Jill Sterkel, the USA's team captain and most seasoned veteran, swimming on her fourth Olympic Team, might have raised a concern. But none did.

In a *Sports Illustrated* article from Seoul, writer Craig Neff quotes retired USA Olympic coach Don Gambril in referring to East German star Kristin Otto: "She is certainly one of the greatest swimmers of all time," Gambril said. "She reminds you of Tracy Caulkins." [103]

If Gambril, Schubert, Quick, or Jill Sterkel, all of whom had tremendous credibility within the sport, were not willing to speak up with their suspicions, then who would? It seems the USA, with only circumstantial evidence in the observable physical side effects, chose to follow the lead that George Haines had set more than a decade earlier.

Four decades after Montreal, Schubert admits, "We knew that they were doping. But none of us had the balls to speak up." [104]

Sterkel had seen the press skewer Shirley at the '76 Games, so her takeaway was that silence was the best policy in Seoul. But that did not stop her from singing the Star Spangled Banner in her head while the ponderous East German anthem was played during the awards ceremony for the 50 freestyle in Seoul. Ironically, Sterkel shared the podium with three likely steroid-doped athletes, when she tied to the hundredth of a second for the bronze medal. At 27 years of age, as team captain of her fourth USA Olympic team, Jill Sterkel's unlikely third-place finish against two East Germans and a Chinese swimmer was certainly a gold-medal effort.

The only real bright spot for the Americans in Seoul was five-foot five-inch Janet Evans, who beat the steroid-enhanced East Germans in the distance events, winning the gold medal in the 400 and 800 freestyles and the 400 individual medley. Janet's world records in the 400 freestyle and her 1989 world record in the 800 freestyle are among the longest standing world records in swimming history and earned her the nickname Miss Perpetual Motion. When Evans won her first of three gold medals for the USA, it marked the first time a female American swimmer had beaten an East German in an individual Olympic event since Munich in 1972.

Interestingly, a look at the record book during the East German doping era from 1973 through 1988 shows that the 400 freestyle and 800 freestyle records were the hardest ones for East Germany to acquire. Only two East Germans held the 400 or 800 freestyle record times during this fifteen-year period. By contrast, East Germans held the world record for the 100 freestyle for the entire fifteen-year doping period. Common sense would say that extra muscle mass and power and the subsequent additional body weight associated with the type of steroids the East Germans were using were not as conducive to enhanced performance in longer, more aerobic events.

The East German doping program prevailed through the 1988 Games and was decidedly more sophisticated by the Seoul Olympics. East Germany's Kristin Otto won an unprecedented six gold medals in Seoul. At the time, there was no 4x200 freestyle relay event for women. Had there been one, Otto would almost certainly have matched Mark Spitz's seven gold medals from the Munich Olympics.

Of course, Kristin Otto, the most decorated woman Olympic swimmer of all time, and Kornelia Ender, who won four golds and one silver at Montreal, are reluctant to attribute their Olympic success to Oral Turinabol. They know firsthand the incredible sacrifice and hard work, steroid-enhanced or not, that they endured to achieve their Olympic success.

Petra Thumer, the most open of the German swimmers from 1976 freely admits steroid use, but in the same breath implies that swimmers from the USA may have been doping as well.

In the filming of the USA Swimming documentary *The Last Gold*, NBC producer Brian Brown addresses this question out of journalistic integrity. He asks the question directly to those who would be in a position to know the best. Colorado Springs, Colorado attorney Rich Young, sums up the perspective of the group of experts who were interviewed.

"Do you believe that any of the USA women from the '76 team were using steroids?"

"I've been working in the antidoping area for 30 years now, and I would be highly, highly surprised if any of the US women were doping based on the context and everything else I know." [105]

Kornelia Ender, Kristin Otto, Petra Thumer and as many as 12,000 other former East German athletes are among "the generation of the Wall," as victim advocate Ines Geipel describes.

"As a group, we have always hoped that the stars of East Germany would also talk about it, and indeed talk about their stories in concrete terms. That's never happened—Kristin Otto, Kornelia Ender, many others haven't done it.

"From a psychological standpoint, one can understand why [they won't admit to doping], but for those victims who will not get their lives back, it was naturally very hard to experience," Geipel says. "For twenty years we've had these documents that have laid it all out, but those who have been damaged have always been publicly discredited here in Germany."[106]

It is hard to make all the connections and say definitively that the instances of liver cancer, birth defects, and other major health issues that appeared in some of the East Germans women decades later were a direct result of the steroids, but Ines Geipel and the survivors strongly suspect the correlation. What is clear is that many former East German athletes are dealing with debilitating health issues that will plague them to the end of their lives.

Almost ten years after the fall of the Berlin Wall, German prosecutors brought charges against many of the coaches, trainers, and doctors who carried out the doping program. These trials were significant, according to Dr. Franke, because of the elite status afforded medical doctors in the nation of Germany. It was one thing to convict a former swimming coach of doping underage athletes, but quite another to bring allegations forward in a public trial and convict a doctor of what was essentially a charge of child abuse.

At Dr. Lothar Kipke's trial, Michael Lehrner, the German attorney for the victimized athletes, compared Kipke with the Nazi Josef Mengele, known as the Auschwitz "angel of death." [107] But Dr. Kipke remained unapologetic for his role in the doping program. Sports historian Andrew Strenk, who had known Kipke since 1968, recalls the elderly doctor's defiance even after his conviction in German court. Far from regretting his involvement in doping children for the glorification of the East German state, Lothar Kipke was still proud of his achievements and kept meticulous records of the doping program in his home office in Leipzig, remembers Strenk.

In 1989, Christiane Knacke, the first woman to break 60 seconds in the 100 butterfly, admitted to using steroids during her career as an elite East German swimmer. In 1991, a group of twenty coaches from the former East Germany signed a letter admitting to the use of performance enhancing drugs. Despite these admissions and the documentation recovered by Dr. Werner Franke and Brigitte Berendonk, as of 2016, the 40th anniversary of the Montreal Games, the International Olympic Committee has refused to adjust the results from Montreal or to award duplicate medals to the women who placed behind East German athletes.

In the continuing fight against performance enhancing drugs, the International Olympic Committee would form the World Anti-Doping Association (WADA) in November 1999. The USA would follow in 2000 with the creation of the United States Anti-Doping Association (USADA).

Colorado Springs attorney Rich Young, who helped guide the formation of the USADA, has been on the front lines of the anti-doping battle since its earliest days. As an attorney and father of children involved in athletics, he is clear on the need to preserve sport from those who would suggest that athletes should be able to dope if they accept the risks involved.

"You hear debates about just [letting] everybody dope. That isn't what sports are about. There is a reason we have sports in our schools, and we don't have circus in our schools," Young says. "It's the lessons you learn from sport—how to win with grace, how to lose with grace and learn from it, how to be a good teammate. If the lesson from sport is, well, you need to cheat to win, then we shouldn't have sport in schools. I should immediately switch my kids from sport to piano lessons," Rich Young says with some irony. "That's why I have been doing what I do for the last twenty years and have such admiration for Dr. Franke and Brigitte." [108]

In a complete change from the East German doping era, USA coaches finally broke their silence when they suspected wide-scale doping of Chinese athletes at the 1994 World Championships in Rome. Dennis Pursley, then director of the USA national team, and John Leonard executive director of the American Swim Coaches Association, rallied the coaches and wrote a letter of protest to FINA. The coaches from the USA, Australia, and other countries held a press conference and laid out their suspicions before the international press.

"Dennis Pursley and I looked at each other and said, 'We've seen this happen before [in East Germany] and we are not going to let it happen again on our watch,'" Leonard remembers.

According to Leonard virtually every nation in attendance signed the letter of protest. "Basically we said we believe we have a rogue nation exactly like the East Germans and, having learned from the East Germans, we demand that FINA take action." [109]

Chapter 17

BRIGHT FUTURE FROM A DARK PAST

NEITHER KORNELIA ENDER nor Petra Thümer swam in another Olympics. In 1978, Thümer learned for the first time about the doping of East German athletes and that she herself had been doped with steroids. After the realization, there were times when she would spit out her steroid pills in the water during warm-up.

"I wanted success," she says, "but I did not want to come by success in the wrong way." After retirement, she became a commercial photographer. Today, she swims daily with old friends and teammates in the same pool where she grew up training in Karl Marxstadt.[110]

In 1992, Kornelia Ender acknowledged she knew about the doping. But nowadays, in a complete turnabout, she tries her best to deflect questions about it. "There is no doubt in my mind that I did not of my own free will take part in any doping, and if so, someone must have given it to me somewhere," she says. "I took no pill that I could conclude (was doping)—blue or whatever fit the description afterward. I can't say if they gave me something. I don't know. My coach is no longer alive."

After Montreal, she achieved unprecedented acclaim back at home. However, Ender quickly ran afoul of the East German elite when she abruptly quit swimming. She intended to go into university training to become a doctor. But after flatly refusing to continue to train and compete, the medical school training never materialized. Today, she works with athletes as a physiotherapist. [111]

The future for the American relay swimmers in Montreal was a mixed experience of the old paradigm and the new frontier. Wendy Boglioli was the only swimmer to clearly speak out about the suspicions of steroid use by the East Germans. In a New York Times article after the Montreal Games, Wendy said she suspected steroid use. "I don't think it should come to taking male hormones and steroids in order to compete," she said. [112]

She was promptly terrorized. Ominously, newspaper clippings of the victorious USA relay team with crude and obscene drawings on the photos were mailed to Wendy and her husband, Bernie. The pictures were sent simultaneously from five different U.S. cities on the same day. The harassment was so well organized and premeditated that the FBI started an investigation. The young couple lived a few months in fear and changed their home phone number before things settled down.

Wendy swam one more summer, ended her career with a spectacular dual meet rematch between the USA and East Germany in 1977. She set American Records in both the 100 butterfly and 100 freestyle. At the dual meet held in Berlin, the next wave of young American swimmers—Tracy Caulkins, Sippy Woodhead and others who were rising to lead the USA—affectionately nicknamed the twenty-two-year-old

Boglioli "Grandma."

Kim Peyton, one of the early stars of women's collegiate swimming, never slowed down. To understand Kim, it may be best to look toward the end of her life. In 1979 with an aggressive brain tumor growing on her right frontal lobe, she convinced her doctor to postpone exploratory surgery and radiation until after her championship meet in March. As the collegiate champion in the 200 free and anchor for all of Stanford's relays, she knew the team needed her.

For some reason, perhaps her omnipresent sunny outlook and goodwill, the state of Oregon had embraced Kim from a very young age. In track-and-field-obsessed Oregon, Peyton had gone head to head in 1974 with Oregon track star Steve Prefontaine for a prestigious Oregon Sportsman Award.

"Prefontaine is pretty good," Peyton's coach, Don Jacklin, said at

Kim Peyton's family, sister Debbie, dad Gene, mom Barb and sister Kelly with a portrait of Kim. *(Photo credit: Barbara Peyton)*

the time, "but he's no Kim Peyton." Jacklin pointed out that Kim had three American Records, two World Championship medals, and three Pan American Games Championships to her credit.

Of course, Prefontaine achieved legendary status, in part because of his tragic early death, but in light of the legacy of the 4x100-free relay that Kim and her teammates won in Montreal, it is easy to agree with Jacklin now. To this day, Kim Peyton is the greatest amateur athlete the state of Oregon can claim.

While the reach of Title IX stretched well beyond sport, nowhere was it more visible to the American public than in the area of college sports. In practical terms, Title IX effectively forced colleges to provide the same intercollegiate athletic programs to their female students as to their male students. Provisions to include facilities, scholarships, competitive schedules, professional coaching staffs, and the financial resources to support these new programs were all implied in the application of the law.

The change was not immediate, as university athletic departments struggled to reapportion resources, but over the next twenty years, women's collegiate swimming grew exponentially. Well-funded programs at major universities from north to south and east to west revolutionized collegiate swimming for women. By the turn of the century, the women's NCAA Championship meet was, like the men's meet, the most competitive swim competition from top to bottom held anywhere in the world, even compared to the Olympic Games.

Of the USA relay members from Montreal, Jill Sterkel benefitted the most from the implementation of Title IX. In 1979, she signed a full scholarship to swim at the University of Texas. In a storied career, Sterkel amassed more collegiate championships than any other swimmer in history. At the mid-point of her career at Texas, Jill was nine for nine in winning collegiate championships and was awarded the prestigious Broderick Cup as the nation's top female collegiate athlete. By her senior year, Sterkel would win an astounding twenty-one collegiate championships, including sixteen individual titles and five relay titles.

Over the years between Montreal and Seoul, Jill Sterkel would also become the heart and soul of the USA women's team internationally. She was elected team captain for the 1980, 1984, and 1988 USA Olympic teams. She ended her international career with two Olympic gold medals on the 4x100-free relay in Montreal and Los Angeles, and an individual bronze medal in the 50 freestyle in Seoul.

Jill Sterkel on the podium after the 50 freestyle final at the Seoul Olympics 12 years after Montreal.
(Photo credit: USA Swimming)

In what must have been among the greatest recruiting classes of women athletes, Shirley Babashoff and Kathy Heddy both signed with UCLA after Montreal. With Babashoff and Heddy on the squad, the UCLA Bruins were the odds-on favorite to go 1-2 in every freestyle event from the 100 to the mile—and Kathy was the best 200 IM swimmer in America just for good measure. But coach Colleen Graham's joy was short-lived when

Shirley retired after one semester. She was just plain tired of swimming, Shirley explained to *Swimming World*.[113] Unfortunately, Kathy never fully recovered from the back injury that plagued her in the summer of 1976. So she swam only one collegiate season before retiring.

After retiring from swimming, Babashoff traveled the world for a time promoting a swimwear company with Mark Spitz. While flight attendants immediately sought to upgrade Spitz to first class, Shirley was hardly recognized. In every instance, Mark Spitz kindly introduced Babashoff and requested an upgrade for her as well.

Shirley determined to live the "normal" life that she desired during her moments of doubt before the Olympic Trials in 1976. In sunny Southern California, these days she is nearing retirement from the U.S. Postal Service. The greatest joy and accomplishment of her life is not a relay gold medal, she says, but being a mom. When someone suggests that her life was "stolen" from her, she is adamant that she's had a good life out of the limelight, living the joys of motherhood and uncomplicated work. But it is clear that a certain future was taken from her.

In all probability, without the doped East Germans in the races, Shirley would have been the Olympic champion in five events: the 200, 400, and 800 freestyle, along with both relays, the 4x100 medley and the 4x100 freestyle. Returning to an adoring American public with five gold medals, she would have landed in the same category as Mark Spitz—pulled into the limelight and cherished in the public eye long after Montreal.

"She should have been up there on the Wheaties box," Montreal teammate Camille Wright points out. "She should have been an American hero." [114]

Back in Mission Viejo, new Animals emerged and the Animal Lane thrived for another decade. Mark Schubert's team eventually eclipsed his hero George Haines' record of forty national championships, winning forty-three before Schubert moved on to higher profile coaching positions. He oversaw the USA's most elite athletes as the national team director for USA Swimming from 2006 through 2010, including the 2008 Beijing Games of Michaels Phelps' incredible eight gold medals.

"In Montreal, there were no winners," reflects *The Last Gold* producer Brian Brown in an interview with Mark Schubert almost forty years after the Games. Without pause, Schubert makes the obvious correction: "Except," he says, "in the 400 freestyle relay."

Kim Peyton, Wendy Boglioli, Jill Sterkel, and Shirley Babashoff stand at the pinnacle of a rich history of women's swimming dating back to Ethelda Bleibtrey and the first USA Olympians in Belgium, fifty years before Montreal.

In one of her most lucid and unguarded moments with the press corps in Montreal, Babashoff seemed to grasp the collective power of the team that had pulled off the impossible victory. In the post-relay interview, her last race completed and the intense pressure of the week at Montreal suddenly removed, she shrugged off the implication of relief in a reporter's question about finally winning a gold medal.

"I guess I just needed a little help from my teammates," she simply said.

Shirley Babashoff, standing on the starting block in Montreal in her stars and stripes skin suit and signature black goggles, also stood at the edge of a new age of women's swimming in America. With Jill Sterkel thrashing into the lead, and one untarnished gold medal on the line, Shirley took one deep breath, then another, and swam into history.

Brian Goodell, Mark Schubert, and Shirley Babashoff back home in Mission Viejo after Montreal. *(Photo credit: Brian Goodell)*

ABOUT THE AUTHOR

KEITH "CASEY" CONVERSE has been coaching women's swimming in the NCAA for more than 30 years. His teams at the United States Air Force Academy have accumulated more than 300 dual meet wins and two NCAA Division 2 Championships during his tenure.

As an athlete, Converse swam on the USA's 1976 Men's team in Montreal, finishing 12th in the 400 freestyle. The following year he became the first person to swim the 1650 under 15 minutes, winning the NCAA Championship and setting the American Record for the University of Alabama.

With more than four decades observing the sport of swimming as an athlete and coach, Converse is in a unique position to reflect upon the obstacles facing the USA Women's team in the revolutionary era of international swimming between the Munich Games and Montreal.

In 2014 Converse served as Technical Consultant for the USA Swimming documentary *The Last Gold*, which chronicles the lead up to the Montreal Games and the epic final showdown in Montreal between the USA women and the East Germans in the 4x100 freestyle relay.

Contact the author at kcconverse@munichtomontreal.com.

APPENDIX A

10 Best Women 100 Freestylers in the World

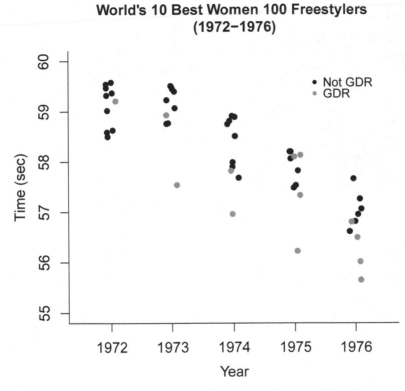

Credit Chris Bramer | The Counsilman Center for the Science of Swimming at Indiana University

World's 10 Best Women 100 Freestylers
(1972–1992)

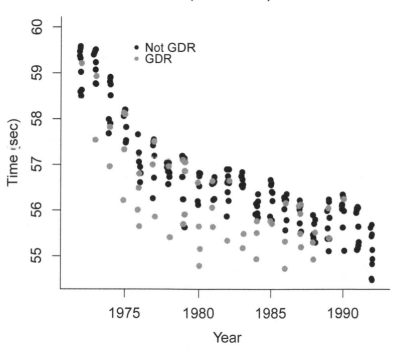

Credit Chris Bramer | The Counsilman Center for the Science of Swimming at Indiana University

APPENDIX B Corrected Results From the 1976 Women's Olympic Swimming Competition

100 Freestyle

Gold	Enith Brigitha	Netherlands
Silver	Kim Peyton	USA
Bronze	Shirley Babashoff	USA

200 Freestyle

Gold	Shirley Babashoff	USA
Silver	Enith Brigitha	Netherlands
Bronze	Annelies Maas	Netherlands

400 Freestyle

Gold	Shirley Babashoff	USA
Silver	Shannon Smith	USA
Bronze	Rebecca Perrott	New Zealand

800 Freestyle

Gold	Shirley Babashoff	USA
Silver	Wendy Weinberg	USA
Bronze	Rosemary Milgate	Australia

100 Backstroke

Gold	Nancy Garapick	Canada
Silver	Wendy Hogg	Canada
Bronze	Cheryl Gibson	Canada

200 Backstroke

Gold	Nancy Garapick	Canada
Silver	Nadiya Stavko	Soviet Union
Bronze	Melissa Belote	USA

100 Breaststroke

Gold	Lyubov Rusanova	Soviet Union
Silver	Marina Koshevaya	Soviet Union
Bronze	Gabrielle Askamp	West Germany

200 Breaststroke

Gold	Marina Koshevaya	Soviet Union
Silver	Maryna Yurchenya	Soviet Union
Bronze	Lyubov Rusanova	Soviet Union

100 Butterfly

Gold	Wendy Boglioli	USA
Silver	Camille Wright	USA
Bronze	Wendy Quirk	Canada

200 Butterfly

Gold	Karen Thornton	USA
Silver	Wendy Quirk	Canada
Bronze	Cheryl Gibson	Canada

400 Individual Medley

Gold	Cheryl Gibson	Canada
Silver	Becky Smith	Canada
Bronze	Donnalee Wennerstrom	USA

400 Medley Relay

Gold		USA
Silver		Canada
Bronze		Soviet Union

400 Freestyle Relay

Gold		USA
Silver		Canada
Bronze		The Netherlands

Final Medal Count

	USA	Canada	Soviet Union	Netherlands	Australia	New Zealand
Gold	7	3	2	1		
Silver	3	5	4	1		
Bronze	4	2	2	2	1	1
TOTAL	14	10	8	4	1	1

CASEY   BILLY   TAYLOR   LONSDALE   JIMMY

Cassandra Elaine Dixon
mamacass@carbonmade.com

SOURCES

Chapter 1
1 Shirley Babashoff, USA Swimming interview, August 2014
2 Bob Ingram, "US Nationals," *Swimming World,* May 1976, page 28
3 Donna de Varona, USA Swimming interview, August 2015

Chapter 2
4 Peter Daland THE HISTORY OF OLYMPIC SWIMMING Vol 1: 1896-1936, (Colorado Springs, CO, USA Swimming Press, 2009), page 55. Daland notes that the reason for the surprising improvement in swimming speed in Antwerp was due in large part to the historic change in swimming technique from the trudgeon—a combination of crawl arm stroke combined with a scissors-kick—to traditional freestyle utilizing the flutter kick.
5 Shirley Babashoff, USA Swimming interview, August 2015
6 Simon Reeve, *One Day in September,* (New York, New York, Skyhorse Publishing, 2000) page 2

Chapter 3
7 Al Schoenfield, "First World Championships," *Swimming World,* October 1973, page 8
8 Kim Peyton, Personal letter to her family from Belgrade, Yugoslavia, September 1973
9 Jean Pierre LaCour, translated by Nick Thierry, "Why are the East Germans so Good?" *Swimming World,* October 1973, page 33
10 Al Schoenfield, "First World Championships," *Swimming World,* October 1973, page 8

Chapter 4
11 Jurgen Weber, *Germany,* (Budapest, Hungary, Central European University Press, 2006) page 2
12 Jurgen Weber, *Germany,* (Budapest, Hungary, Central European University Press, 2006) page 7

13 Henry Kirsch, *The German Democratic Republic, The Search For Identity* (Boulder Colorado, Westview Press, 1985) page 165

14 Jurgen Weber, *Germany*, (Budapest Hungary, Central European University Press, 2006) page 67

15 Brigitte Berendonk, USA Swimming interview, July 2014

16 Ines Geipel, USA Swimming interview, Berlin Germany, July 2014

17 Dr. Werner Franke lecture, American Swim Coaches Association Newsletter, 2012, Edition 12, page 6

18 Steven Ungerleider, *Faust's Gold* (New York, NY, St Martin's Press, 2001) page 57

19 Werner Franke, USA Swimming interview, Heidelberg Germany, July 2014

Chapter 5
20 Al Schoenfield, "US Nationals," *Swimming World*, May 1974, page 6

21 Coach Jack Simon, email message to the author, July19, 2012

Chapter 6
22 Al Schoenfield, "Nationals," *Swimming World*, September 1974, page 33

23 Bob Ingram, "Dual Supremacy," *Swimming World*, October 1974, page 6

24 Jurgen Weber, *Germany*, (Budapest Hungary, Central European University Press, 2006) page 62

25 Bob Ingram, "Dual Supremacy," *Swimming World*, October 1974, page 6

26 Bob Ingram, "Dual Supremacy," *Swimming World*, October 1974, page 7

27 Cecil Colwin, "Taking Stock in Concord," *Swimming World*, October 1974, page 14

28 Karen Moe-Thornton, author interview, Omaha, Nebraska, July 2012

29 Cecil Colwin, "Taking Stock in Concord," *Swimming World*, October 1974, page 14

30 Cecil Colwin, "Taking Stock in Concord," *Swimming World,* October 1974, page 14

Chapter 7
31 Ines Geipel, USA Swimming interview, Berlin, Germany, July 2014
32 Ines Geipel, USA Swimming interview, Berlin, Germany, July 2014
33 Ines Geipel, USA Swimming interview, Berlin, Germany, July 2014
34 Andrew Strenk, USA Swimming interview, California, August 2014
35 Jurgen Weber, *Germany,* (Budapest Hungary, Central European University Press, 2006) page 1
36 Dr. Werner Franke lecture, American Swim Coaches Association Newsletter, 2012, Edition 12, page 9

Chapter 8
37 Al Schoenfield, "World Champiohsips: An Analysis," *Swimming World,* September 1975, page 110
38 Jack Ridley, author phone interview, April 2014
39 Al Schoenfield, "The Big Swim at Cali," *Swimming World,* September 1975, page 6
40 Bob Ingram, "Women's Events," *Swimming World,* September 1975, page 50
41 Al Schoenfield, "World Championships: An Analysis," *Swimming World,* September 1975, page 110

Chapter 9
42 Bob Ingram, "Confucius Analyzes Nationals," *Swimming World,* May 1976, page 112
43 Wendy Boglioli, author interview, Omaha, Nebraska, July 2012
44 Bill Palmer, author phone interview, July 2012
45 Enith Brigitha, author interview, Santa Clara, California, August 2015
46 Karen Crouse, USA Swimming interview, October 2014
47 Robert Page, "Swimmer Electrocuted at Park," Falls News Press, June 1971

48 Shirley Babashoff, USA Swimming interview, August 2015
49 Shirley Babashoff, USA Swimming interview, August 2015

Chapter 10
50 Drew McDonald, USA Swimming interview, May 2015
51 Bob Ingram, "U.S. Olympic Trials," *Swimming World*, July 1976, page 35

Chapter 11
52 Ashley Harrell, "Jack and Diana," *Broward New Times*, June 14, 2007
53 Bob Ingram, "U.S. Olympic Trials," *Swimming World*, July 1976, page 38
54 Karen Moe Thornton, author interview, Omaha, Nebraska, July 2012
55 Jim and Bev Montrella, author interview, Omaha, Nebraska, July 2012
56 Carolyn Finneran, "Commentary," *Swimming World*, March 1974, page 15
57 Kenny Moore, *Sports Illustrated*, July 13, 1992
58 Frank Elm, author phone interview, July 23, 2012
59 Karen Moe Thornton, author interview, Omaha, Nebraska, July 2012
60 Karen Moe Thornton, author interview, Omaha, Nebraska, July 2012
61 Jill Sterkel, author phone interview, May 2012
62 Dick Pound, USA Swimming interview, May 2015
63 Lethbridge Herald, July 26, 1976
64 Bob Ingram, "U.S. Olympic Trials," *Swimming World*, July 1976

Chapter 12
65 Bob Ingram, "Relays," *Swimming World*, September 1976
66 John Naber, USA Swimming interview, August 2014
67 Steve Gregg, ABC Television broadcast, July 18, 1976
68 Bob Ingram, "Carlile on American Swimming," *Swimming World*, October 1974, page 14
69 Karen Moe Thornton, author interview, Omaha, Nebraska, July 2012

70 Bob Ingram, "U.S. Olympic Trials," *Swimming World,* July 1976, page 37
71 From Rueters, "E. German Swim Champ Ill, Out of Olympics," *Los Angeles Times,* July 9 1976, page E2
72 Jerry Kirshenbaum, "Theirs Was A Midas Stroke," *Sports Illustrated,* August 2, 1976
73 Bob Ingram, "Butterfly Events," *Swimming World,* September 1976
74 Bob Ingram, "Freestyle Events," *Swimming World,* September 1976
75 Steven Ungerleider, *Faust's Gold,* (New York NY, Thomas Dunne Books, St Martin's Press) page 45
76 Jean Pierre LaCour, translated by Nick Thierry, "Why Are the East German's So Good?" *Swimming World,* October 1973, page 33
77 Bob Ingram, "Freestyle Events," *Swimming World,* September 1976
78 Bob Ingram, "Butterfly Events," *Swimming World,* September 1976
79 Joe Gergen, USA Swimming interview, August 2015
80 Joe Gergen, USA Swimming interview, August, 2015
81 Shirley Babashoff, USA Swimming interview, August, 2014

Chapter 13
82 Brent Rutemiller, *Swimming World,* audio, 2007
83 Brent Rutemiller, *Swimming World,* audio, 2007
84 Jill Sterkel, author phone interview, 2012
85 Shirley Babashoff, USA Swimming interview, August 2015
86 Bob Ingram, "Backstroke Events," *Swimming World,* September 1976
87 Bob Ingram, "Freestyle Events," *Swimming World,* September 1976

Chapter 14
88 Jim and Bev Montrella, author interview, Omaha, Nebraska, July 2012
89 Craig R. Whitney, "East Germany Spurs Athletes to Olympian Heights," *The New York Times,* December 21, 1976 page 39

90 ABC Television broadcast, July 25, 1976

Chapter 15
91 ASCA recording, September 1986
92 Craig Lord, "Sporting Crime of The Century," American Swim
Coaches Newsletter, November 2009
93 Geoffrey Miller, "Three Athletes Disqualified For Using
Drugs," Associated Press, July 31 1976
94 Rich Young, USA Swimming interview, May 2014
95 Brigitte Berendonk, USA Swimming interview, July, 2014
96 Ines Geipel, USA Swimming interview, July 2014
97 Dr. Werner Franke, USA Swimming interview, July 2014
98 Dr. Werner Franke, USA Swimming interview, July 2014
99 Brigitte Berendonk, USA Swimming interview, July 2014

Chapter 16
100 ASCA recording, September 1976
101 John Leonard, author interview, July 2015
102 Jay Fitzgerald, author interview, August 2015
103 Craig Neff, "Swim Six, Win Six," *Sports Illustrated Vault*,
October 1989
104 Mark Schubert, author interview, August 2015
105 Rich Young, USA Swimming interview, May 2014
106 Ines Geipel, USA Swimming interview, July 2014
107 Michael Lehrner, USA Swimming interview, July 2014
108 Rich Young, USA Swimming interview, May 2015
109 John Leonard, author interview, July 2015

Chapter 17
110 Petra Thümer, USA Swimming interview, July 2014
111 Kornelia Ender, USA Swimming interview, July 2014
112 Gordon S. White, "A Woman Swimmer Returns With Medals, Bad Memories," *The New York Times*, July 29, 1976, page 15
113 "Babashoff Retires," *Swimming World*, January 1976, page 8
114 Camille Wright, USA Swimming interview, October 2014